THE CONFLICT OF THE AGES

The Conflict of the Ages

THE MYSTERY OF LAWLESSNESS:
ITS ORIGIN, HISTORIC DEVELOPMENT
AND COMING DEFEAT

BY

ARNO CLEMENS GAEBELEIN, D.D.

PUBLICATION OFFICE "OUR HOPE"
(Arno C. Gaebelein, Inc.)
456 Fourth Avenue, New York, N. Y.

PICKERING & INGLIS
14 Paternoster Row
London, E. C.

Glasgow, Scotland

H. L. THATCHER
135 Symonds Street
Auckland, N. Z.

G. F. ARDILL
145 Commonwealth Street
Sydney, N. S. W.

KESWICK BOOK DEPOT
315 Collins Street
Melbourne, Australia

All Booksellers in U. S. A.

33-37443

TABLE OF CONTENTS

The Conflict of the Ages

CHAPTER I

The Great Enigma

The marvelous universe with its countless stars and distant nebulae, the earth upon which man dwells, animate and inanimate creation, life itself, and above all, human existence and destiny—these are all a great enigma. For thousands of years members of the race, endowed with the faculty of reasoning, the capacity to search and to explore, have raised certain questions. Some answers have been found, yet the most vital questions have not been answered in the past and, in spite of the boasts of certain scientists, they remain unanswered today.

What is the origin of this almost infinite space we call universe? How did it all come into existence? How did the laws which govern and uphold the different solar systems with an astonishing precision, perfect and inerrant, originate? Is our earth the only planet on which life is flourishing? How did life originate on our globe? What is man? What is the future of the earth? What is going on in these heavens so deep and so mysterious? What is in existence beyond the farthest point reached by the most powerful telescope? These are a very few of the many questions which have baffled scientific efforts and which constitute the great enigma.

There are plenty of theories which attempt and propose a solution. Many times certain cocksure scientists have announced triumphantly their discoveries, assuming that at least a part of the riddle had at last been solved. But soon after their findings, other scientists, by their research, have proved the supposed solution incorrect and another exploded hypothesis has been buried in the ever-growing graveyard of forgotten scientific theories.

Human science—what is it? We let another answer with well-chosen words. "It is, as we know only too well, an edifice composed of light and darkness, of truth and error, of humble research and arrogant dogmatism, of daring hypothesis and clearly demonstrated theories, of millions of facts and billions of thoughts, of the inborn and the acquired, of yes and no, of dreams of the past and the future, of unbending prose and high-flown poesy; an edifice continually being built up, now slowly, now quickly, and in constant need of repair, ever growing, yet never completed."*

What ludicrous things have been taught and are being taught by these scientists who ridicule the faith of Christians, who push aside God's revelation found in His Word, and who arrogantly assume that direct Creatorship according to Holy Scriptures is incredible! Their theories make the greatest demand upon man's credulity.

We mention but one still advocated by a number of scientists. They say that the simplest forms of life were carried and are carried through space by tiny particles and picked up in some unexplainable way. These particles containing life-germs were carried by meteorites to our globe. This explains the existence of all life found on our earth, in a drop of water, or in the unsearchable depths of the sea, animal life in thousands upon thousands of varieties, and also human life. But a meteorite rushing through space becomes a fiery, a red hot, mass. How then could a little speck of life have survived such an intense heat? Only a miracle can account for such a survival. And tell us, O ye scientists, where did these dust particles, carrying the life germs, come from? The denial of an omnipotent creator postulates the self-generation of these dust particles. Another unbelievable miracle.

As this is not a work dealing with the different theories of science and pseudo-science, endorsed by modernism of the religious stamp—theories which are the stock in trade of the different brands of atheism—we do not cite other equally ludicrous assumptions which do not come anywhere near the solution of the great enigma.

Yet one thing needs to be said—all these theories have

---

*Prof. Bettex, "Science and Christianity," page 191.

one common trend. They uphold a spontaneous generation. Dead matter, they say, was always existing, hence it must be eternal. They do not believe in the existence of an eternal Being, God, but they believe in the eternity of matter, call it protoplasm or by any other name. This dead matter was quickened into life by natural law. Life called thus into existence by spontaneous generation gradually shaped itself into manifold and marvelous expressions, culminating in the race of human beings. Therefore not only matter is self-made, but natural law, also, is self-existent; it developed itself, endowed itself without any outside influences, with super-intelligence, producing all the marvelous things in nature—things so great that man is unable to comprehend them. To offer as a solution of the enigma of life, such theories as these—dead matter producing life, and life shaping itself into hundreds of thousands of different forms, through self-made laws, devoid of free will—is a gross insult to the intelligence of any human being. Nature reveals everywhere astonishing designs. Over a hundred years ago Dr. Paley wrote his "Natural Theology" in which this great scholar uncovers the marvels of the human body and some of its delicate organs like the eye and the ear, at the same time tracing other equally amazing designs in other spheres of life. His arguments demolish the whole infidel theory of chance and blind laws. What a blessing it would be if this master-work could be republished and put into the hands of our youth, to save them from the high school and college parrots, who still prattle and babble over long-exploded theories.

Louis Agassiz, the great scientist, started out as an atheist. After progressing in his scientific research, he became deeply convinced that his atheism was a miserable, a lying invention. The study of nature led him to nature's God and he became a believer and an earnest worshipper. Nor is he the only eminent scientist who has acknowledged the superiority of the supernatural knowledge offered to man in the Bible. There are many others. One of the noblest words spoken by the great scientist, Lord Kelvin, is the following: "We are absolutely forced by science to believe with perfect confidence in a Directive Power—in an influence other than physical or dynamical or electrical forces." And now, after certain infidels have had their say for several decades as to spontaneous generation and these mysterious laws of nature, the leading, the foremost, scientists of our times are almost in unison that the rule of blind law in nature can no longer be maintained.

Dr. Fitchett, in his lecture on "The Unrealized Logic of Religion" says: "It were as easy to believe that, say, Milton's 'Paradise Lost,' had been set up in all its stately march of balanced syllables by an anthropoid ape, or that the letters composing it had been blown together by a whirl-wind, as to believe that the visible universe about us—built upon mathematical laws, knitted together by a million correspondences, and crowded thick with marks of purpose—is the creation of some mindless Force."* And the late Professor Francis Bowen of Boston, Massachusetts, a great thinker, has left us the following declaration: "I have faithfully studied most of what the philosophy of these modern times, and the science of our own day, assume to teach. And the result is, that I am now more firmly convinced than ever, that what has been justly called the 'dirt philosophy' of materialism and fatalism is baseless and false. I accept with unhesitating conviction and belief the doctrine of a being of one personal God, the Creator and Governor of the world, and of one Lord Jesus Christ, in whom dwelleth all the fulness of the Godhead bodily; and I have found nothing whatever in the literature of modern infidelity, which, to my mind, casts even the slightest doubt upon that belief."

One of the greatest materialists of the nineteenth century was Ernest Haeckel. An ardent defender of the spontaneous generation hypothesis, he uttered a sentence which is of much significance. He said: "If we do not accept

---

*The author is indebted for this and other quotations to the excellent volume by Prof. Dr. Theodor Graebner, "God and the Cosmos," a work which we cannot recommend too highly.

the hypothesis of spontaneous generation we must have recourse to the miracle of a supernatural creation." In other words, when the spontaneous generation theory is disproved, the only other alternative is direct creation. Not so long ago much was being said by certain boasting scientists that they were on the high road of producing life artificially. Among the most loud-mouthed was a certain Professor Loeb. He tried to manufacture living cells out of some slimy matter. We do no longer hear of such foolish attempts, because true scientists know the truth, *"Omne vivum ex vivo"*—"all life from life." Pasteur and Tyndall have given the death-blow to the spontaneous generation invention. And all materialists should ponder over one of the last utterances of the famous Lord Kelvin: "It is impossible to conceive either the beginning or the continuance of life without an overruling creative power. I feel profoundly convinced that the argument of design has been greatly too much lost sight of in recent zoological speculation. Overpoweringly strong proofs of intelligent and benevolent design lie around us, showing to us through nature the influence of a free will, and teaching us that all living things depend on one everlasting Creator and Ruler."

Scientist after scientist has expressed his opinion that spontaneous generation cannot be proved and is nothing but a myth. Professor Conn, in his "Evolution of Today" (page 26) says: "There is not the slightest evidence that living matter could arise from non-living matter. Spontaneous generation is universally given up." And years before, another eminent searcher, M. de Quatrefages reached the following conclusions: "I make bold to affirm that the deeper science penetrates into the secrets of organization and phenomena, the more does she demonstrate how wide and how profound is the abyss which separates brute matter from living things." In view of such outspoken declarations of real scientists, the words of H. G. Wells, in his "Science of Life," appear puerile: "As a matter of history, life on this planet originated not from life." But how weighty and significant are the words of the co-worker of Charles

Darwin, Alfred Russell Wallace: "So marvelous and so varied are the phenomena presented by living things, so completely do their powers transcend those of all other forms of matter subjected to mechanical, physical, or chemical laws, that biologists have vainly endeavored to find out what is at the bottom of their strange manifestation and to give precise definitions, in terms of physical science, of what life really is." Thales, six hundred years before Christ, expressed his belief that all life originated in sea-water. Materialists have travelled the same road and now, over 2500 years after, are not nearer the solution of the origin of life. The Darwinian Evolution is dead, a thing of the past, and all the other materialistic theories are on their death beds. Men of real scholarship acknowledge readily that the enigma of the beginning of life remains unsolved. They admit very frankly that spontaneous generation remains, and will always remain, an unproved theory.

Let us listen to just a few of them. Professor William Bateson of Cambridge, one of the greatest biologists, says: "It is impossible for scientists longer to agree with Darwin's theory of the origin of species."

Dr. W. H. Thompson, former president of the New York Academy of Medicine, declared "The Darwinian theory is now rejected by the majority of biologists as absurdly inadequate."

Dr. Etheridge of the British Museum, the leading authority on fossils, says: "Nine-tenths of the talk of evolutionists is sheer nonsense, not founded on observation, and wholly unsupported by facts. This museum is full of proofs of the utter falsity of their views."

Here are the words of Professor Beale of King's College, London: "In support of all naturalistic conjectures concerning man's origin, there is not at this time a shadow of scientific evidence."

And Herbert Spencer, an outstanding evolutionist, made the fatal admission that: "No scientist of repute ever claimed that evolution is science. It is only an unproved hypothesis."

Professor Huxley said: "Evolution, if consistently believed, makes it impossible to believe the Bible." And Professor Drummond—who was a professed Christian and who had fallen for evolution—before he died declared: "I am going back to the Book to believe it and to receive it, as I did at first. I can no longer live on uncertainties."

Professor Virchow, who was one of the foremost medical men and scientists, said: "It is all nonsense. It cannot be proved by science that man descended from the ape or any other animal. Since the announcement of the theory, all real scientific knowledge has proceeded in the opposite direction."

Another Englishman, Sir Charles Bell of London, made the statement: "Everything declares the species to have their origin in distinct creation."

An eminent German zoologist, Professor Fleischmann of Erlangen, adds his testimony by saying: "The Darwinian theory of descent has in the realm of nature not a single fact to confirm it. It is not the result of scientific research, but purely the product of imagination."

We realize that few scientists today, though evolutionists many of them, are no longer Darwinians. The point is that Darwin's five causes of evolution—survival of the fittest, heredity, variations, struggle for existence and natural selection—are admitted by men like Bateson and others to be impossible as causes of evolution. Yet, while Darwinism is as dead as it can be, evolution persists. Many leading biologists confess their total ignorance as to the cause of evolution, yet they still believe in it.

Therefore we have said: "Darwinism is dead and all other materialistic theories are on their death beds." Yet, in spite of these facts and the increasing demonstrations that Darwinism and spontaneous generation are unscientific—totally unproved—high school teachers and college professors, male and female, continue to teach the young the lies and deceptions of Darwin—paving for our youth the way which leads into atheism, radicalism and immoral lawlessness. And words fail us when we think of the so-called *"clergymen"* who pose as "Christian leaders," who have violated their ordination vows and who brazenly hiss forth these lies as scientific facts. If they had a drop of honest blood in their veins they would drop their Christian profession, disown their affiliation with evangelical denominations, and accept the invitation of "Free-thinkers" and "Atheists" to join hands with them in the attempted destruction of the Truth of God.

Inasmuch, then, as spontaneous generation is dead and gone—an exploded theory (as Ernst Haeckel said)—supernatural creation remains as the only alternative. But who is going to give us light and understanding as to supernatural creation? Who is going to answer satisfactorily the age-long question as to the origin of all things? True it is spontaneous generation being inadmissible and impossible furnishes indirectly the proof of a direct creation. But this is not satisfactory. We need something more positive. Can it be obtained by more research, by more powerful microscopes and telescopes? Is man, by searching alone, going to solve the great enigma? Or is there another channel through which the needed knowledge, the knowledge which science is unable to bestow upon us, may be obtained?

Without a moment's hesitation we answer this question affirmatively. The human race has at its disposal a supernatural knowledge given in a supernatural way. This knowledge which offers to man the Truth is positive, fixed, unchangeable, unaffected by the changing things of time. It is a knowledge which transcends human reason, a knowledge which is offered to man to believe. Scientific knowledge is only deduction and as such nothing but sinking sand. But this higher knowledge is not gained by reasoning deductions, but by acceptance of faith. Well said Emanuel Geibel: "The end of philosophy is to know that we must believe."

But who has this super-knowledge to offer? Where does it come from? The knowledge which brings to man the

Truth and the solution of the great enigma comes from the Almighty Creator, God Himself. It is divine revelation knowledge.

According to David, the illustrious King of Israel, it is only the fool who says in his heart "There is no God" (Psa. xiv:1). This was written by David three thousand years ago. Even at that time men were living who were mental perverts and attempted the denial of the existence of a Being by whom all seen things were made. The King who lived a life crowded with the evidences that God is—who had fellowship with Him, had received messages by His Spirit, was led and preserved by Him—brands the atheist a fool. Belief in God, as the author has shown in another volume (*), is a universal fact in the human race. Polytheism, fetishism, animism, and other forms of paganism, have for a basis belief in the unseen and in supernatural beings. Nor is polytheism (the worship of many idols) the original form of worship, which, according to evolution, man adopted when he came forth from his animal ancestry. Far from that! The most painstaking and scholarly anthropologists have brought to light that monotheism, the belief in one God, was the belief of the human race at one time. They knew God, the Creator of heaven and earth, in the beginning. The atheist is contra-natural; he belies his own consciousness. Atheism is a mental obsession, a mental perversion; it denies what demons cannot deny. "Thou believest there is one God; thou doest well, the demons also believe and tremble" (James ii:19). It is no compliment to our civilization when men and women, cultured and uncultured, learned and unlearned, turn to atheism. It is not progress but one of the outstanding evidences of degeneration.

A God, who created all things, whose offspring man is, demands a revelation.

Man cannot know God by himself. God must come down to man and reveal Himself to His creature. "Canst thou

---

*Christianity or Religion?"

by searching find out God? Canst thou find out the Almighty to perfection" (Job. xi:7).

That God has revealed Himself in His creation is an unquestionable fact. "The heavens declare the glory of God and the firmament showeth His handywork. Day unto day uttereth speech, and night unto night showeth knowledge" (Psa. xix:1-2). "The visible things of Him from the creation of the world are clearly seen, being understood by the things that are made, even His eternal power and Godhead" (Rom. i:20). All nature bears witness to the existence of an Almighty God, who has manifested His Omnipotence and His Wisdom everywhere. The greatest scientists are not the materialists, the atheists, but men who believed in God, for they discovered His footprints in creation. Copernicus, the founder of the great system which made his name immortal, was a godly man. He requested to have put on his tombstone the words: "That which Thou hast granted the dying thief is all I ask." Kepler, an equally great astronomer, whose discoveries are as great as Newton's, concluded his most important work with these words: "I thank Thee Lord, Creator, that Thou hast given me this joy in Thy creation, this delight in the works of Thy hands. I have proclaimed the glory of Thy works to man as far as my finite mind was capable of grasping Thy infinity. If I have said anything which is unworthy of Thee, or if I sought after mine own honor, forgive me." Sir Isaac Newton, whose discoveries still are unsurpassed, in spite of the claims of a certain infidel, was a diligent student of the Bible and a firm believer in its infallible Truths. Linneaus, the greatest naturalist of all times, when discovering inflorescence, cried out with delight: "I have seen the footprints of God." William Herschel, another great astronomer, said: "The wider the field of science extends, the more numerous and indisputable become the proofs of the eternal existence of a creative and almighty wisdom." Leibnitz, one of the most powerful thinkers, was a believer, the author of a beautiful hymn: "Jesus, whose death and suffering have brought us life and joy." One of the greatest chemists was

Liebig. He unreservedly and joyfully confessed his faith in God and said: "The chief value and glory of science is that it promotes true Christianity."

Among the more recent astronomers, Maedler holds a high rank. He made the statement: "A true student of nature cannot be an unbeliever; natural law and God's law are one and the same." Similar confessions have come from the lips of Faraday, Robert Mayer, Agassiz, Pasteur, Lavoisier, Cuvier and many others.

We quote but one more, who is, we believe the greatest living American scientist, Professor R. A. Millikan, of California. He writes in his "Science and Life" (page 56): "It seems to me as obvious as breathing that every man who is sufficiently in his senses to recognize his own inability to comprehend the problem of existence, to understand whence he himself came and whither he is going, must in the very admission of that ignorance and finiteness recognize the existence of Something, a Power, a Being, in whom and because of whom he himself lives and moves and has his being. That Power, that Something, that Existence, we call God."

Still more outspoken are the words of Professor Shepardson, an electrical engineer of International reputation, who says: "The evidence obtainable from study of material phenomena gives us confidence in concluding that a Supreme Being exists, that He is profoundly intelligent, that He designed and constructed and governs the universe, and that He encourages those who seek to learn of His works and ways."*

But there is a higher source from which this knowledge springs. God has revealed Himself in and through His *Word*. While Creation reveals Him in His Omnipotence, in His Wisdom, and all Creation makes known His Glory, the great enigma is not solved by these things.

When Walter Scott, the well-known novelist and poet, was approaching the end of his life, he requested his son-in-law to bring to him the book. The son-in-law asked the

---

*"The Religion of an Electrical Engineer."

dying man, "What book?" Sir Walter answered: "There is but one Book—the Bible."

Countless thousands have found out that when it comes to dying that there is only one book. That Book is rightly called "The Book of books." We have no time or space to waste with the refutation of the coarse and perverted attacks which present day atheist and free-thinkers have launched against the Book. Nor do we pay attention to the more subtle attacks which are so widespread in Christendom itself, which masquerade under the name of Bible-Criticism. The atheist openly and boldly stabs the Bible with his dagger; the baptized infidels in the different evangelical denominations betray the Bible with the Judas kiss.

Frequently the writer has been asked for a substantial reason of his unswerving faith in this Book as the infallible revelation of God, in which the things unknowable by scientific research are made known. The answer he gives is—the Bible itself. We have read and studied this Book for over sixty years. With many millions of human beings, among them the most noble of the highest intellect, we, too, have found that this Book contains in its blessed pages the words of eternal life and brings to the mind and heart the knowledge which satisfies and gives assurance. The more the great Book is read and searched the more the conviction grows that it is not an empty, unmeaning, human phraseology which the chosen instruments, who produced its pages, wrote several thousand times: "Thus saith the Lord," and "The Word of the Lord came unto me," and again "The Lord spoke unto me." The more one turns in the spirit of reverence to this Book the stronger becomes the conviction that the Book is "God-breathed."

The holy men of God wrote as they were moved and controlled by the omniscient Spirit of God. The sixty-six books which compose the Bible were written by different men under different circumstances yet they present a supernatural unity, which can only be explained by the one supernatural author. We compare it to a magnificent structure resting upon an unmovable rock. As we enter the portal and explore the structure we discover marvelous things. As we climb higher and higher the vision enlarges; through its windows we look over the distant past and before us spreads the panorama of the future, till we reach the great capstone, the final great revelation, from which we behold human destiny in the endless ages of eternity.

The real scientist, not the scienticulist with a smattering of picked-up knowledge, sees God's footprints in all Creation. In a far higher sense the true student of the Bible can trace God's footprints in all history, learn from it what Being He is, find here His majestic and infinite attributes. He is seen in His Omnipotence, as the Eternal One, in His Omniscience, in His Omnipresence; He is Light, Holiness and Righteousness, He is Love, all-merciful, the God of Mercy and of Grace. This is the unsurpassed glory of the Book—God—Revelation. Human reason cannot comprehend Him; the finite can never reach up to the infinite. Faith accepts Him and finds in the knowledge of Him the help, the comfort, the joy and peace, which no science is able to give.

But the Bible also reveals the origin of man, solves the enigma of human existence and makes known human destiny. Here we receive the knowledge that man is not like the beast that dies, that he is not evolved from the beast, but is a created being in a class by himself. In him is the breath of the Almighty, he possesses endless being. Between the lowest man and the highest developed beast is therefore a gulf which cannot be bridged. All attempts to find the missing link are hopeless. How can one find a thing which does not exist?

And this Book with its super-knowledge, with its solution of the great riddle, is hated and despised today as never before. Yet in spite of all the hatred, all the pernicious attacks to destroy the Book, or to undermine its authority, the old Book stands. It will continue to stand for God and His Word are One. So let the turbulent, the turbid and the angry waves of atheism, modernism and other forms of infidelity dash with increasing force against the Rock of Ages. The waves will cast up their own mire and dirt, only to be broken to pieces. The Rock will stand.

Unspeakably majestic is its beginning. "In the beginning God created the heavens and the earth." This one sentence, composed in the Hebrew of seven words silences forever the invented theories of man and annihilates the false religious inventions with which man tries to satisfy his religious instinct.

Here is the complete and final answer to materialism and spontaneous generation. The different forms of agnosticism are refuted; atheism is given the lie, and polytheism and pantheism are wiped out by these seven words.

The charge is brought against the Bible that it fixes Creation as having taken place some six thousand years ago. The Bible does not make any such claim. The date put over against the first verse of the Bible in some editions— 4004 B. C.—is put there by man. It is no part of the inspired text. The age of the physical earth is not revealed in God's Word and science gives only the wildest guesses. Perhaps the reason why this is not revealed in the Bible is that no human figures could express the age of our globe.

But what is the meaning of the second verse of Genesis where we read that the earth was without form and void, or as it should be translated, waste and empty? Geology gives us an interesting information in connection with this mysterious chaos. It reveals the fact that originally this earth existed in a different form from what it is today. It once sustained a gigantic animal creation and an equally gigantic vegetation. Something happened to this prehistoric earth. It was plunged into death and destruction; a great cataclysmic change took place. It remained in that condition for an incalculable period of time during which the earth was submerged in water and probably covered with ice. What happened to the original earth? Why did the Creator let it go down into the night of death?

In our next chapter we shall touch briefly on the possible solution of this mystery. From the Creation account we learn that God in His own time, and that was but recently, dispelled the darkness by light, commanded the light to shine out of darkness, and commanded the earth to come out of the state of death on the third day. The earth is garnished once more with vegetation and a new animal world is called into existence.

It is interesting to find that the word "create" is used thrice in the first chapter of the Bible. It is found in the first verse in connection with the beginning of all things, when God created out of nothing. It is found in the twenty-first verse in connection with the new animal Creation and finally it is used in connection with the creation of man. The other word used is "made." This necessitates the existence of matter, which is shaped into something. So God put the earth into the condition as the dwelling place of an intelligent being. That being is man.

What dignity God's Word puts upon man! God speaks in the plural, because while He is One, there is with Him in all eternity His Word and His Spirit.

"And God said, Let us make man in our image, after our likeness, and let them have dominion over the fish of the sea, and over the fowl of the air, and over the cattle, and over all the earth, and over every creeping thing, that creepeth upon the earth. So God created man in His own image, in the image of God created He him; male and female created He them." Man's constitution is more minutely given in the second chapter of the Bible. "And the Lord God formed man from the dust of the ground, and breathed into his nostrils the breath of life, and man became a living soul." It is this which differentiates man from the beast. Man is the offspring of God. If these opening chapters of this Book are not true, then throw your Bible away; it begins all with a lie! But if there is a beginning, as there is, a God, a heaven, and an earth, and man the offspring of God, then the Bible is true to the last word concerning the new heaven and the new earth.

And man is seen in fellowship with His Creator. He is not described as a half-ape only uttering grunts without intelligent language. The first man possessed a higher intelligence than man possesses today. God showed to

Adam, His created beings, every beast and every fowl, to see what Adam would call them. "And Adam gave names to all cattle, and to the fowl of the air, and to every beast of the field." Let us suppose that Mars is inhabited and possesses an animal creation adapted to that planet. Let us suppose that in some way a Committee of Scientists headed by H. G. Wells and Albert Einstein were suddenly transported to Mars and confronted with the different animals found on that planet. Would they be able to name them in as correct a way as Adam did? Certainly not. Adam possessed the knowledge of God's creation, the knowledge now lost to man, which he tries to recover and which eludes his grasp. But something happened to man. The fellowship, the great purpose of man's existence, was broken. The mystery of lawlessness was born. The tragic history of the human race begins; it is still being written as never before.

But even the Bible, the written Word of God, is not the very highest revelation of God, in which knowledge is offered and the great enigma is solved. There is a higher revelation. It is the revelation of God in His Son, the eternal Word of God, known in history as the Lord Jesus Christ. The Bible had announced His coming. Prophet after prophet had by divine inspiration written of His person and of His work. He appeared and entered human existence in the supernatural way of the Virgin Birth, conceived by the Holy Spirit. He came to make the invisible God visible in His Person. "No man hath seen God at any time; the only begotten Son, who is in the bosom of the Father, He hath declared Him" (John i:18). "All things were made by Him, and without Him was not anything made that was made. In Him was life and the life was the light of men" (John i:3-4). "This is the true God and the eternal Life" (1 John v:20). His own words of self-witness confirm these and other statements. "I and the Father are One" (John x:30). "He that hath seen Me hath seen the Father" (John xiv:9). He spoke of His works as a witness of His Deity. Omnipotence and Omniscience were constantly displayed in His life among men.   His moral character manifests holiness and righteousness; God's Love and Mercy are revealed in Him.   In his words of truths He confirms the revealed facts as to God, the origin of man and human destiny.   But the highest purpose of the manifestation of God in the person of His Son, the eternal Word, was the solution of the mystery of lawlessness, to redeem man, to bring man back to God, to reveal the Love of God and ultimately defeat the forces of evil, to dethrone lawlessness and bring all things back to God.

The solution of the great enigma is found in the Person and Work of the Son of God and in the great revelations of the Spirit of God, who has come to show to man the marvelous truths of redemption, the ultimate goal of human existence and all in Him "in whom are hid all the treasures of wisdom and knowledge." Evolution and any other materialistic science has failed to explain His supernatural Person. It can never explain Him. All it can do is to negate.

CHAPTER II

The Origin and Mystery of Lawlessness

"O Lord, how manifold are Thy works! in wisdom hast Thou made them all; the earth is full of Thy riches" (Psa. civ:24). "O Lord, our Lord, how excellent is Thy Name in all the earth! who hast set Thy glory above the heavens" (Psa. viii:1). These beautiful words and many more were written three thousand years ago in praise of the Creator and of His works. All creation witnesses to His majestic greatness, to His Omnipotence, and in all the marvelous designs we can read His wisdom, the wisdom past finding out and also discover His Benevolence.

Yet as we look about us in God's creation, though we see the evidences of His greatness, His wisdom and His glory, we discover that there is evil present. All Creation is marred. It is filled with groans and moans. Something happened which dragged down this good creation. The Apostle Paul, with his inspired pen, wrote of it: "The creature was made subject to vanity—for we know that the whole creation groaneth and travaileth in pain together until now" (Rom. viii:18-22). What are its groans? Earthquakes, tidal waves, disastrous storms, tornadoes, cyclones, a thousand different plights and a thousand other disturbances. And here is man! Called to be the lord of creation, to have dominion over all, we find that he, the offspring of God, created in His own image, is in a far more deplorable condition than the creation which he was to rule. What pen is able to picture the misery, the unhappiness, the sorrows of the human race! What sufferings and corruption we behold! There is a constant struggle for existence. In Scripture nations are compared to the sea, the ever surging, restless, moaning sea. As long as history has been written it records nation against nation, kingdom against kingdom, wars, rebellions, upheavals, disaster upon disaster, no peace, no happiness. We find the oppression of the poor, the sufferings of millions, never able to satisfy their physical needs, in a state of semi-starvation, homeless, in constant pain and

hopelessness. On the other hand the many wealthy with
their greed, ever reaching out for more, to add houses to
houses, land to land, prosperous and deliberately closing
their hearts against the cries of the needy. Autocratic governments which rule in unrighteousness, enslaving the people,
and the people rising up against injustice. Civil wars,
hatred on all sides, class wars, all kinds of corruptions and
hundreds of other things fill the pages of history. Then
the individual hating and hateful, filled with the different
kinds of lust; suffering from disease, and finally passing away
—death ends his conflicts, and the struggle for existence is
over. And what more could we write about crimes, viciousness, certain things unknown in the animal creation below
man.

*Where does it all come from? Who has brought about this
deplorable condition? Who IS responsible for it? What is
the origin of evil and what is the mystery of lawlessness?*

What answer does science give? What has the Darwinian hypothesis, or any other evolution theory to say?

Darwinism and materialism trace it all to the animal
ancestry from which man, according to evolution, sprang.
It is all here by chance, and the evil which originated with
the protoplasm must work itself out gradually, hence the
human race must constantly make for better things, the evils
must become less and less, till finally it has worked itself
out completely. But though this process has been going on,
according to scientific guessings and surmisings, a hundred
million years, more or less as you please, evil today is
manifesting itself in greater power than ever before. There
is more lawlessness in the world today than in any previous
age. In fact, as we show in this volume the whole world
is steeped in lawlessness and all civilization is approaching
an almost inconceivable disaster.

If the evolutionists were right, and God has anything to
do with the imagined protoplasm, then He Himself would be
responsible for the origin of evil. All evil would then be
unavoidable and therefore *excusable*.

The shallow-thinking atheist takes hold of this invention

and tries to make coin out of it.   With blasphemies unknown
before, the twentieth century atheists blame God for everything.   In our own country they issued a call to celebrate
thanksgiving day and called it "Blame giving day service."
They composed a doxology suitable to their perverted
mentality and sang—

> "Blame God from whom all cyclones blow,
> Blame him when rivers overflow,
> Blame him who swirls down house and steeple,
> Who sinks the ships and drowns the people."

From these scientific-atheistic ramblings, we turn to the
sure knowledge given to us in the Bible.   Does the Bible
throw any light on the origin of evil and the mystery of
lawlessness?   If we would have to say—no, this book is
silent about it, then we would be justified in pushing it
aside and we could no longer believe that it is the book
which gives the satisfactory and trustworthy revelation of
God, the knowledge unattainable by human research.

Let us see then what the Word of God reveals as to the
evil which is in the world.

As stated in our opening chapter, man is not the product
of chance, he is not the product of evolution, but the direct
creation of God, in a class by himself.   Darwinism and
evolutionism claim that, coming out of an animal ancestry,
man developed physically step by step.   It has no place
nor explanation for the soul, that gift bestowed by the
Creator to man.

"What is soul according to the Darwinian idea?   A
featureless, characterless, an immaterial but formless
protoplasm, a substratum difficult to define; all distinctions
between good and bad, pure and impure, talented and
stupid—individualities cease—that is they are only passing
wavelets on a sea of unconsciousness—have no permanent
and consequently no real worth.   This view pushed to its
logical conclusion, denies the continuance of individual
existence, therefore the immortality of the soul."[*]

*Bettex, "Science and Christianity," page 135.

But this is not true. More and more does archaeology disprove the whole invented scheme. The late Professor A. H. Sayce, whose scholarship was of the very highest wrote:

"Ever since the establishment of the doctrine of evolution it has been assumed that man started like a child and slowly grew into what he is today. Our primitive ancestor has been seen again in the modern savage, whose nearest representative he has been held to be. The brain and mentality of civilized man, it has been assumed, have developed out of small beginnings; he started almost on a level with the brute beasts and has become a Newton or a Napoleon. But here again archaeology stands in the way. The men who carved the hardest of stones into living portraitures in the Egypt of six thousand years ago, or at a later period erected the Parthenon at Athens, were in no way inferior to the most gifted of ourselves. We have accumulated more knowledge, it is true, but we can claim no superiority in the powers of mind. And if we go back to a still earlier age, the record is the same. The marvelous carvings and drawings of paleolithic man of the Aurignacian age prove that on the artistic side there has been little, if any, development. Indeed when we consider the conditions under which his work was done, in a climate like that of Greenland and amid the darkness of subterranean caves, we are inclined to regard him as the greatest artist humanity has produced."*

Such arguments as these wipe out the assumptions of a certain class of men who claim to be scientists, but lack in real scholarship. Archaeology has even furnished far greater facts against the Darwinian evolution, since Dr. Sayce wrote these words.

Perhaps the greatest philologist who ever lived was another Oxford professor of a generation ago, Dr. Max Müller. His works like "Science of Language," "Chips of a German Workshop," "Philological Essays," and many more are monuments of human learning. Comparing language with language, he furnished another conclusive argument for the Biblical revelation that man is the intelligent creature, the direct creation of God and not a developed beast.

"As far as we can trace the footsteps of man even on the lowest strata of history, we see that the Divine gift of sound and sober intellect belonged to him from the very first; and the idea of humanity emerging

*Introduction to "Wonders of the Past," page 6.

slowly from the depths of an animal brutality can never be maintained again in our century (the nineteenth). The earliest works of art by the human mind—more ancient than any literary document, and prior even to the first whisperings of tradition—the human language, forms one uninterrupted chain, from the first dawn of history to our own times. We still speak the language of the first ancestors of our race; and this language with its wonderful structures, bears witness against such gratuitous theories. The formation of language, the composition of roots, the gradual discrimination of meanings, the systematic elaboration of grammatic forms—all this working which we can see under the surface of our own speech attest at least from the very first the presence of a rational mind, of an artist as great, at least, as his work."*

There is in the last book of the Bible a beautiful outburst of praise. The Creator-Lord is addressed and we read: "Thou hast created all things, and for Thy pleasure they are and were created" (Rev. iv:2). This is true of man. God created man for His own pleasure, for His fellowship.

God is holy, He is Light and in Him is no darkness at all (1 John i:5). He dwells in an unapproachable light (1 Tim. vi:16) and therefore creating in His own image and likeness, He did not produce a being of darkness and evil.† He cannot be the Creator of evil. The creature He called into existence, man, was innocent; He was made a moral being endowed with intelligence. As a moral being he possessed freedom of will and was conscious of it. This freedom includes possible independent action. But could he be allowed to exercise this free will in his own way? We answer, No. He must be, as a moral, free being, subject to the controlling will of God. There was therefore an absolute necessity that God assert His control over man as His moral creature. This demands obedience. So God gave to the first man a decisive rule for action which demanded his voluntary and unconditional submission as a moral free agent to God's righteous requirement. Law means restraint—expressed by the words "thou shalt not"; it means to give up independence of action; it demands sub-

---

*"Essays," Vol. I, page 306.

†"I create evil" (Isa. xlv:7), does not mean moral evil. It means the punitive actions of the righteous God.

mission. So God revealed the fact that His creature is subject to His will. A test is given. "And Jehovah God commanded the man, saying, Of every tree of the garden thou mayest freely eat; but of the tree of the knowledge of good and evil, *thou shalt not* eat of it, for in the day thou eatest thereof thou shalt surely die" (Gen. ii:16-17). We are not concerned here with giving a definition of the tree of the knowledge of good or evil. Nor do we know how long Adam and the woman remained in this state of innocence. As stated in the previous chapter Adam revealed his super-intelligence by giving names to the living creatures of the earth. For an undefined period they enjoyed fellowship with their maker. There was nothing to mar it. Walking in submission to the will of God all was peace. But the test had to come; it had to be made.

The third chapter of Genesis reveals the test. Here we find the birth of evil as far as the human race is concerned. Let modernists sneer and infidels mock, but this chapter which records the tragedy of man's failure and fall, changing him from an innocent creature to a guilty one, is one of the deepest and most instructive portions of the Bible.

A new actor appears upon the scene. It is a person who uses one of the creatures as an instrument. Behind the serpent, then a different creature from the serpent of today, stands an unseen person of speech and intelligence. He is not a friend of God, but an enemy. He is crafty. His craftiness is revealed in that he selects the woman for the object of his attack. The law "thou shalt not" was given to the man; no doubt the man passed it on to the woman. The tempter may have reasoned that the man having heard the Creator's voice and demand, might not respond. The first he does is to create in the mind of the woman distrust. Has God really spoken, has He said, "Ye shalt not eat of every tree in the garden?" The woman, instead of turning away from such a suggestion, yielded. Then comes the lying assertion that self will, breaking through the restraint, disobeying God, would bring freedom and self-gratification through exaltation. "Your eyes will

be opened, and ye will be as God, knowing good and evil."
The act is committed. Sin is born and according to Bible
definition *"Sin is lawlessness"* (1 John iii:4).*

But who is this being who comes to make the test? Who
is this enemy of God? Who is he who succeeds in making
of an innocent creature a rebel? Where does he come from?
A multitude of questions can readily be asked and while
they are not completely answered in the Bible itself, enough
light on this person is given which has satisfied the reason
of the most intelligent, the deepest thinkers of the race.
And what is not known, which our reason craves to know,
the true Christian believer in submissive humility acknowl-
edges as unrevealed mystery, withheld for some all wise purpose.

Above man is another world, the world of a higher order
of beings, the angels of God. They are the tenants of the
universe and have access to that which is above the heavens. †

They were created, we do not know when. Perhaps it
was when the earth was founded, after the heavens had been
created, for we read in connection with creation: "When
the morning stars sang together and all the sons of God
shouted for joy" (Job xxxviii:7). There are different ranks
in that angelic world above. Among these great beings
was one who is mentioned in Scripture as "Lucifer, the son
of the morning" (Isa. xiv:12). Lucifer means "Brilliant
Star" or "Lightbearer." He was originally one of the
greatest and most majestic creatures of God. Like man
all angels also were created moral beings with freedom of will.
Something happened in pre-historic times at a period of
time which is unrevealed and therefore unknowable. Lucifer,
the great creature of God, and the angels also had a "Thou
shalt not." Then Lucifer, who may have been one of the
archangels, became a transgressor. Other angels took
part in the rebellion and so he became the author of the first
lawlessness, the author of sin. Much is hidden from us,
and God has not been pleased to lift the veil which hangs

---

*This is the correct translation; the authorized version is faulty.
†For a complete treatise consult the author's "The Angels of God."

over the first tragedy of the universe. Yet if we turn to the
Scripture passage where Lucifer, the son of the morning, is
mentioned, we find more than the statement of his fall.
The words which that great being spoke, which led to his
fall, are on record. He said in his heart—"*I will* ascend
into heaven, *I will* exalt my throne above the stars of God.
. . . *I will* ascend above the heights of the clouds; *I will*
be like the most High" (Isa. xiv:13, 14). Here is the language of self-will, self-exaltation. The Creator had given
to Lucifer and the angels under him a fixed abode. He was
not satisfied with it. He aimed at heaven itself. God
had given him a throne; he wanted that throne above the
stars of God. He aimed higher and reached out after the
place of God Himself. Perhaps he may have seen the
eternal Son of God, by whom and for whom God had created
all things, and moved with envy and jealousy he aspired
to be in His place.

Can we possibly locate the original habitation of this
mighty angel? It was a place covered with clouds, for he
desired to ascend "above the clouds." We cannot speak
dogmatically about it, but inasmuch as this globe existed
once with a gigantic creation, and judgment came upon it,
plunging it into death and chaos, it is not unreasonable to
draw the conclusion, that the original earth must have been
the part of the universe where Lucifer had his throne.
Certainly the judgment by which the original earth was
visited postulates a reason. Here we must leave it.

It would be useless to follow the philosophical and theological discussions about this being and his fall. Nor can
man with his finite reason grasp the infinite One and understand His thoughts and ways. "For as the heavens are
higher than the earth, so are my ways higher than your
ways, and my thoughts than your thoughts" (Isa. lv:9).
Some have tried to solve the problem by saying that God
ordained sin and lawlessness for His own glory, that He
might by means of it, illustrate the perfection of His own
character—His justice in punishment and His mercy in
pardon. Such a theory slanders the character of God.

Infidels and atheists scoff at all this.   One of their common
questions is: "If God is omniscient and knew beforehand
that such a being would become a rebel, the devil, why did
He create him at all?"   True believers acknowledge that
God has not revealed all, and that they look into a glass
darkly, know only in part.   We must trust God.   We know
that all His ways are perfect, all-righteous and all-wise, and
that the day is coming when we shall know as we are known.

In Christendom, that portion of it which is rationalistic,
the fallen Lucifer, the enemy of God, the source of evil, of
sin and lawlessness, is branded a legend.   They claim it is
a belief which the Jews picked up in Babylon.   But what
about the second Man, our Lord, who met that being in
person?   What about His teachings in which He mentions
that sinister being as the murderer from the beginning and
the father of lies?   "Ye are of your father the devil, and the
lusts of your father ye will do.   He was a murderer from
the beginning, and abode not in the truth, because there is
no truth in him.   When he speaketh a lie, he speaketh of
his own, for he is a liar, and the father of it" (John viii:44).
We are told by the modernist that the Lord Jesus Christ
either did not know any better than to believe what His
superstitious contemporaries believed, or if He knew, He
accommodated Himself to their beliefs in order not to
antagonize them.   By such statements they deny the in-
fallibility of the Son of God and make of Him a mere human
being or a hypocrite.

Such, then, is the origin of sin, according to the Word of
God.   It was by the one man, the first Adam, that sin came
into the human race and death by sin (Rom. v:12).   How
terse the statement yet how deeply significant: "Adam begat
a son in his own likeness, after his image" (Gen. v:3).   And
so human history is now generation after generation, "conceived and born in sin"; the reign of lawlessness and death
begins.   The unseen, dark being, who had lost his dominion
now reaches out after it through fallen man, whom he induced
to share his own rebellion.   He had lost his throne but

through man's lawless act he becomes once more "the prince of this world."

Before the first man was expelled from the presence of His creator, he had to hear the terrible results of his act of disobedience. Curse and sorrow and all that goes with it have come, and finally "dust thou art, and unto dust shalt thou return" (Gen. iii:17-19).

Yet something far greater preceded this announcement of fallen man's future history. Jehovah-God speaks for the first time in prediction. "And I will put enmity between thee and the woman, and between thy seed and her seed; it shall bruise thy head, and thou shalt bruise his heel" (Gen. iii:15). It is one of the most marvelous verses in this great Book. We take a tiny little seed and plant it somewhere. Out of it springs forth the tree with its sturdy trunk, its many branches, with hundreds of twigs, and thousands of leaves. This verse is the seed of all prophecy. In it we find contained the great majestic tree of divine prophecy and revelation with its thousands of prophecies, promises and their realization.

The words are addressed to the sinister being, the erstwhile Lucifer. Two things are prominently stated: There is to be a conflict from now on, a conflict which will go on through the ages, and in the second place the conflict will end in the bruising, or crushing, of the serpent's head. Here is the forecast of history and God's redemptive program, which will end with victory on God's side, the dethronement of evil, the defeat of lawlessness.

CHAPTER III

The Redemption Promise of God and the Beginning Conflict

In His unfathomable eternity, God knew all that would happen in the creation He would bring into existence. All was foreknown by Him. It behooves us to say, "Such knowledge is too wonderful for me; it is high, I cannot attain unto it" (Psa. cxxxix:6). As we have seen, He created all things for His own pleasure. But His purpose in creation has been disturbed. The creature He created for His delight and fellowship is now alienated from Him, plunged into lawlessness, in unrest, unhappiness, and under the curse; death rules. But that does not mean the defeat of God. God can never be defeated. All must end in His glory.

In one of the great New Testament documents we read of "the eternal purpose which He purposed in Christ Jesus our Lord" (Ephes. iii:11). We notice it is an *eternal* purpose. It goes back before the foundation of the world. It is God's purpose of redemption which He purposed when He foreknew all that would take place. It was purposed in a person. The Person is "Christ Jesus our Lord." His name in eternity is "the Only Begotten Son of God."

And right at the threshold of human history, on the scene of man's fall, the beginning of lawlessness, God speaking in prophetic promise for the first time announced Him through whom He would execute His eternal redemption purposes. *The seed of the woman!* That seed is to crush the serpent's head. He is to procure the victory for God over the being of darkness and end sin and its curse. And here is a faint hint, how it is to be accomplished. The heel of the seed is to be bruised; in other words He is to suffer. Such is the germ prophecy of redemption—suffering followed by conquest and glory.

Were we to follow now the age-long unfoldings of God's redemption promises in Scripture we would have to fill hundreds of pages and even this would not exhaust it. The little seed grows into the tree of promise, ever expanding in its heavenward growth.

Prophet after prophet announced Him. A complete picture of His person and His work is revealed throughout the Old Testament Scriptures. He is to come from Shem; He is to be of the seed of Abraham; He is to come from the tribe of Judah and finally He is promised to come from the seed of David. What an unfolding! We read of Him as Immanuel, Jehovah manifested in the flesh, that is, in the form of man. He speaks in the history of the Old Testament as the "I Am"; the prophet announced Him as the Wonderful, the Counsellor, the mighty God, the Everlasting Father and the Prince of Peace. The Spirit of God speaks of Him as "the Son of God" (Psa. ii), in eternal fellowship with God (Prov. viii:22-31). He Himself comes down to man in sacred history, He appears in the form of the Angel of Jehovah and manifests His glory.

His life of humiliation as the seed of the woman is revealed to us in these prophecies beginning with His birth and ending with His suffering, His sacrificial death, His physical resurrection and His ascension to take His place at the right hand of God. He is to come born of the Virgin. His character of lowliness, of holiness and righteousness, His words of grace and His service in the power of the Spirit of God, His miracles, opening the eyes of the blind, making the lame man to leap like a hart, and other works of mercy and power—all and much more is pre-written in the prophetic Scriptures. But most of all His sufferings are foretold. He is to be the man of sorrows, acquainted with griefs, despised and rejected of man. The manner of His death is minutely described a thousand years before it took place— death by crucifixion (Psa. xxii). The suffering and the shame of the Cross, and many other things connected with His death we find in different Scriptures. Historical events and types like the passover-lamb, the sheltering blood, the brazen serpent and others reveal Him and His work. The entire Levitical code of sacrifices and offerings are hundreds upon hundreds of sign-posts all pointing to the one spot— the death He should die. Isaiah the prophet received the great message revealing the fact that His suffering and death would be vicarious. He bears the sorrows, the griefs, the sins of others. He was wounded and bruised not on account of His transgressions, for He never transgressed. Deeper still the announcement that God Himself bruised Him, put Him to grief, made His soul an offering for sin (Isa. liii). We also read that in His burial His body was not to rest in some pauper's or criminal's grave, but that "men appointed His grave with the wicked, but He was with the rich in His death, because He had done no violence, neither was there guile in His mouth" (Isa. liii:9). The fact of His resurrection was announced a thousand years before it happened "His body could not see corruption" (Psa. xvi). Other prophecies announced the same fact of His physical resurrection, which was also typified by the experience of the prophet Jonah. After His resurrection we behold Him ascended on high as revealed in the one hundred and tenth psalm: "The Lord said unto my Lord, sit Thou at my right hand, until I make Thine enemies Thy footstool."*

But this is not the complete divine forecast of the work of the seed of the woman. The same who is predicted to utter that awful word, "My God, My God, why hast Thou forsaken Me?" is to have a kingdom and all the ends of the world shall remember and turn unto the Lord, and all the kindreds of the nation shall worship Him (Psa. xxii:27). He will receive the nations for His inheritance and the uttermost parts of the earth for His possession. The throne of all the earth belongs to the second Man and through Him man's lost inheritance is to be restored. The old serpent, called the dragon, Satan, the devil, will be stripped of his power, so that he can deceive the nations no longer. The seed of the woman, the promised One, in His Kingship will also make wars to cease unto the ends of the earth, and all nations will turn swords into plowshares and spears into

---

*What the death, the resurrection and exaltation of the Christ means, how in it God in infinite wisdom manifests His love and displays the riches of His grace and supplies the lost creature's spiritual need, is briefly stated in the next chapter.

pruning hooks. All strife and hatred will end, all nations
will learn righteousness and dwell together in peace. Poverty
will be gone; the hatred of the ages will cease. Groaning
creation will then stop its groans and begin its singing, for
the curse which sin put here is gone, when the heel of the
seed of the woman has done its work. All this awaits its
fulfillment. And finally there will be a new heaven and a
new earth in which redeemed humanity will dwell for ever
and ever, His tabernacle in their midst, so that God will be
all in all.

We must next look briefly to the announced *conflict*—
the enmity between the woman and the serpent, the seed
of the woman and the seed of the serpent. We have seen
who is meant by the seed of the woman. The serpent is
the author of sin and death. But who is the seed of the
serpent? That part of humanity which sides with this
sinister being and is under his control. According to
Scripture this is true of the entire race in its natural and
sinful state. It is a truth which is almost forgotten in
Christendom today. Does not God's revelation tell us
that the whole world is guilty before God? Is it not written
that the natural man by his sins, his acts of lawlessness, is
dead in trespasses and sins and walks according "to the
prince of the power in the air,"—that is Satan and that such
an one is a child of wrath? (Ephes. ii:1-3). Did not our
Lord say to the Jews in plain words "ye are of your father,
the devil"? Did not John give the same truth when he
wrote the inspired words, "He that committeth sin is of the
devil, for the devil sinneth from the beginning"? (1 John
iii:8). It is a solemn truth! But from the very beginning a
separation took place in the race. It is seen for the first
time in the two sons of Adam, Cain and Abel. Of Cain it is
written, "he was of the wicked one" (1 John iii:12). But
Abel "by faith offered unto God a more excellent sacrifice
than Cain, by which he obtained witness that he was righteous * * *" (Heb. xi:4). Abel was righteous, acceptable
to God, though he was a sinner and shared in his father
Adam's constitution, because he had believed the first

redemption promise. Cain did not believe and thus remained under the dominion of the serpent. This separation in the human race is seen in the first age, the age before the flood. There were the descendants of Seth, the godly, who believed and found grace in the sight of God and the Cainites, who produced in their unbelief a great godless civilization, which ended with a frightful lawlessness; they were the seed of the serpent. In the subsequent history given to us in the Old Testament Scriptures we find these two classes, those who believed God, trusted in Him, falling in line with His eternal purpose, and those who do not believe, who continue in lawlessness and God-opposition under the control of the author of sin and lawlessness; the latter constitute the seed of the serpent. In a sense therefore the God-fearing, promise-believing Israelites, who looked in faith for the coming of the One seed, are also included in the seed of the woman. God accepted them because they believed; like Abraham who believed the promise it was counted to them for righteousness. In anticipation of the redemption work of the Son of God, God was merciful to all who turned to Him with repentance and faith in the coming Saviour and His salvation.

The conflict, then, is the conflict between God and Satan, light and darkness, good and evil, truth and error. But the one great work of the power of darkness is to prevent God from carrying out His eternal purpose of redemption. Serpent-like he strikes at the promised seed and all who are in any way identified with Him. He had heard from Jehovah's lips that his defeat would be accomplished through the seed of the woman. Satan being only a creature is neither omnipotent, nor omnipresent nor omniscient. He did not know when that seed would appear. When the two sons, Cain and Abel, are born to Adam, this intelligent being must have speculated who of the two would be the seed of the woman. Eve had named the first-born "Cain" expressing by this name her belief that he might be the seed, for Cain means, "I have obtained the man from the Lord." When Abel turned to the Lord, believed that first promise

and God's favor rested upon him, the dark being feared he
might be the promised seed and so he used Cain, who on
account of unbelief belonged to him, to kill his own brother.
He is the murderer from the beginning. He was defeated
for Seth took the place of the murdered Abel. The entire
Old Testament history reveals the trail of the serpent. In
every age, in every century, he is seen active through sin,
lawlessness, through violence, rebellion, through lies and
deceptions, now appearing as a roaring lion, and then in the
form of an angel of light, to oppose God, and to frustrate
his purposes.

The Cainites, the descendants of wicked Cain, were his
seed. Under his control they build a great civilization,
erected cities, invented musical instruments, became manu-
facturers and developed agriculture. Every civilization
aims at one thing, to *improve* the world and *better* conditions
and thus eliminate as much of the curse as possible. The
story of that first civilization is the same as that of every
other civilization, including our own. It ended in failure and
increasing lawlessness. With all the inventions and discoveries, different improvements and imagined progress, the
moral conditions became worse and worse, illustrating the
New Testament truth "the world lieth in the wicked one"
and finally the earth was corrupt before God and filled with
violence. Unseen evil powers under the control of the fallen
angel-prince had helped to hasten the terrible corruption
(Gen. vi). That sinister being thought if he dragged down
the human race into God-opposition and defiance, God
would have to destroy it, and thus His purpose of redemption
could not be accomplished. "But Noah found grace in the
eyes of the Lord." Judgment sweeps the earth once more,
the waters of death cover it all, but the ark carries the
eight souls through the judgment waters and a new age begins
in which God continues in the execution of His plans. The
race as a unit had the knowledge of God. They knew Him
by His works and tradition also kept that knowledge alive.
But it was the serpent who filled their hearts with pride
and rejecting the Lord in self-will, to make for themselves

a name, they built the tower. They are scattered and in a short time monotheism gives way to polytheism. They become worshippers of idols and follow the road downward as revealed in Romans i:21-26.

The family of Shem too had followed the drift of the times into idolatry. But God called aside a son of Shem, Abram, whose father, Terah, worshipped idols, and through him God continues the execution of His purpose. To him is promised the seed. And when the promise was made to Abraham, immediately after, the serpent suggested, through Sarai, to produce the promised seed through the Egyptian Hagar.

As we cannot follow the trail of the serpent in all the history of Israel we only give a few more illustrations. Pharaoh's attempt to have the male children of Israel in Egypt killed, was inspired by the murderer from the beginning, and so were all other murderous attempts of history to wipe out the nation from which the seed of the woman was to come. One of the most prominent was the attempt of Haman (Esther iii), who through satanic inspiration had succeeded in appointing the day when the whole nation was to perish.

When it became known that the seed would be a son of David then Satan aims his attacks against the man after God's own heart. Even before David had the definite promise of that son, Satan hated David and would have murdered him through Saul, who belonged to the serpent's seed. A short time after the Davidic covenant had been announced, the dark shadow, getting the knowledge of this covenant, tempted David to sin and the king became an adulterer and a murderer. Satan must have thought that God would be defeated and could no longer use David. Athaliah, the wicked queen, belonged to the Serpent's seed and, under his guidance, she tried to have the seed royal, the offspring of David exterminated. All the wicked kings of Judah and the wicked kings of the ten tribes were linked to the serpent, and through them he attempted to hinder God in the execution of His redemption plan. And what more could we say of the false worship he introduced to corrupt Israel, the idolatrous practises like the worship of Moloch with its horrible sacrifices, the high places, the sacred tree worship, the corresponding moral corruptions which followed and hundreds of other evils which led the chosen people away from God. It was all the serpent's work. The false prophets in Israel, especially in the days of Jeremiah and Ezekiel, the prophets who spoke their own dreams, like the modernistic dreamers of today, promising peace, when there was no peace, were his instruments. He also used the fallen angels, the wicked spirits associated with him, to carry on his work of opposing God and His purposes. He moved David to number Israel in his pride and Solomon, with all his material prosperity and glory, was led by Satan into moral corruption and became a worshipper of idols. Thus he manifested himself as the murderer and liar, to corrupt, to obstruct, to dwarf God's great purpose. God is victor throughout this conflict of over four thousand years. When God's hour arrived, the set time, the appointed time, God sent forth His Son born of a woman (Gal. iv:4).

Throughout these ages of conflict of the serpent and the seed of the serpent, God had in the race those who believed His promises and trusted in Him, who were patiently waiting for the "consolation of Israel" for the coming of the Lamb of God. The serpent hissed at that faithful remnant and would have destroyed them, but they were kept by the power of God.

The other non-Israelitish peoples, the great Gentile nations, who were without Christ (they had no promises of a redeemer) who were strangers from the covenants of promise, without hope and without God (Eph. ii:12), were under the power of the serpent, and through his deception they were led deeper and deeper into darkness and into the abominations of polytheism, with its terrible moral corruptions and atrocities. Some nations even became worshippers of the serpent, and in most of these pagan religious systems, as well as their so-called philosophies, the influences of supernatural evil powers can be traced.

Satan learns of God's purposes through the revealed Word

of God. For the purpose of counteracting God's plan he acquires the knowledge of revealed truth without accepting it.* From the prophetic Word he learned that not only Israel is to have a redemption, but that the Gentiles will receive the light and the ends of the earth shall hear of Him and be saved. In anticipation of all this he instituted the different systems of idolatries and led these nations into the deepest darkness.

*He tempted our Lord by quoting Scripture. Demons who possessed human beings, when Christ drove them out, cried out with fear asking, "Hast thou come before the time to torment us?" thereby revealing a knowledge of what Scripture teaches.

CHAPTER IV

The Victory of God and the Continued Conflict

It is not a mark of superior scholarship and intelligence to reject the fact of prophecy, relating to that promised seed of the woman, and its age-long expansion and development. Prophecy involves the supernatural. Such a minute forecast of a coming person, described in the Old Testament Scriptures, briefly covered in the preceding chapter, postulates a divine omniscience. If this is accepted, the modernistic-rationalistic materialism collapses. We do not enter into the invented theories and attempts to disprove the miracle of prophecy. In the end all confirm the statement of Scripture: "But the natural man receiveth not the things of the Spirit of God; for they are foolishness to him, neither can he know them, because they are spiritually discerned" (1 Cor. ii:14). Some of the explanations are next to incredible. They speak of coincidence, that one should have appeared in whose life these predicted events came to pass, or, that clever men wrote in the Gospels certain things to make them fit to the statements of the prophets, and that the original records were later on embellished by myths and legends to put the halo of Deity around the Person of Jesus Christ. Documentary evidences, research of greater scholars than our materialistic professors, and sound logic prove all these schemes untenable. Prophecy remains one of the miracles of the Book of books.

When the great event took place, and the age long promises, for which generations had patiently waited, were fulfilled, all heaven must have been in wondering commotion. This small earth, one of the smallest bodies in the great universe, as far as we know the only scene of God's redemptive activity, was from the beginning the object of the angel's contemplation. The things of God's redemption the angels desired to look into (1 Peter i:12). They knew that He who had created them, whom they worshipped, would take the creature's form and place, come down from the highest glory, visit the earth, display His glory and carry out God's eternal purpose. So when He was cradled in Bethlehem, He was heralded by an angel and the heavenly hosts broke out in a marvelous praise in which the goal of the redemption God provides is anticipated. On the other hand the serpent also anticipated His coming. All his murderous and lying attempts to keep God back from sending Him came to naught. Step by step the enemy had been defeated. Nor had he the power from keeping Him back in His descent and from overshadowing the Virgin. The seed of the woman and the serpent and his seed are now to be face to face. There is to be a terrific conflict. All the power and cunning of the serpent comes into play in desperate efforts to overcome Him, who is to bruise his head.

Upon the throne in Jerusalem sits, ruling in cruelty, the serpent's seed, Herod. The news reaches him that the "king of the Jews" is born and Gentiles come to seek Him. He knows what that will mean for his own kingdom. He trembles with fear and when the magi do not return, his master, the devil, suggested to him an attempt to reach that child in Bethlehem and to put Him out of existence. The decree is signed and the male children of two years and under were murdered. He whom the enemy sought, who was under the shadowing wing of the Almighty (Psa. xci:1), had escaped.

The Gospel records reveal the fact that at the time of Christ's appearing on earth a large multitude of people were strangely afflicted. They were possessed by demons. Mysterious beings, and often more than one, legions, had taken possession of human beings and ruined them physically and mentally. Such were demon-possessed. Nor is demon possession a myth. It is much in evidence in our own times; our insane asylums are filled from coast to coast with sufferers whose afflictions must be charged to outside evil powers. Missionaries at work in China tell us of the same evil powers; demon possessions are widespread in heathen lands.

We can surmise why that little land of Palestine had such

multitudes of afflicted ones. The serpent wanted to use these demons to hinder the Lord Jesus Christ from carrying out His work. But Christ manifested His power over the demons, and the serpent's efforts were unsuccessful.

When the Lord Jesus appeared to begin His public ministry, there was at Jordan a supernatural manifestation. The divine person of the Spirit came upon Him, a voice was heard from heaven, declaring His Sonship. The serpent, the devil, witnessed it all. Immediately upon that, the Spirit of God led Christ into the wilderness. There He met the author of sin and death face to face. The serpent approached the second Man, not in a garden where everything is beautiful, but in a wilderness among the wild beasts; not in a condition of plenty, with the natural needs of the creature supplied, but in hunger, after the fast of forty days and nights. The serpent comes to make a test. He comes with the things of lawlessness—the lust of the flesh, the lust of the eyes and the pride of life—but he finds nothing in Him. Here is not an *innocent* being, as Adam was, but here is the *Holy One*, Who has no fallen nature. Most interesting and instructive is the last test, when the devil offered to the Lord the kingdoms of this world on the condition that He acknowledge his authority. Two things are notable. The first, the devil claims that the kingdoms of this world are his; such is the case, even to the present time. The second, the serpent anticipated that Christ would ultimately obtain the kingdoms of this world, that He would rid them of lawlessness and the curse through His death on the cross—and therefore He made the suggestion of enthroning Him as the King of kings without the cross and the work the Christ would accomplish there. Most significant! Ever since in the history of the conflict of the present age, Satan tries to build *a Christian civilization without the cross, without that which alone saves and brings back to God.*

And was it not a short time after, that the devil used Peter to suggest to the Lord not to go to Jerusalem to be crucified? The same word our Lord used in rebuking

Satan, He also used with Peter—"Get thee behind me, Satan!"

The different attempts made on His life by the Jews, when they tried to stone Him, or cast Him down a precipice, were inspired by Satan, the serpent. Yet he had no claim on Him, nor could His sinless body be touched by death. All the plans laid to destroy Him, the murderous schemes of the Pharisees and Sadducees, emanated from this sinister being. And how many more times Satan must have tried to ensnare or overcome Him, for it is written after the temptations in the wilderness "he departed from Him for a season" (Luke iv:13).

But we must look deeper into the life and the great mission of Jesus Christ, the Son of God. Why did He come into the world? Why did He take on the form of a servant? To manifest the unseen God? Yes, He did this. To teach and speak words such as were never spoken before? Yes— even His enemies acknowledged this fact. To live the life of righteousness and holiness, which glorifies God, the life the first man might have lived had he not transgressed? Yes—He was perfect in all His ways; no wrong word ever left His gracious lips, nor was there even a sinful thought in His holy mind.

All this is true. But the one great purpose of the coming of the Son of God into the world is something greater than teaching eternal truths, speaking words of eternal life, and living a life which glorifies God. He came that through Him God's eternal purpose in redemption might be accomplished. John states His great work in a most comprehensive way— "*For this purpose the Son of God was manifested, that He might destroy the works of the devil*" (1 John iii:8). It takes us back to Genesis iii:15—the bruising of the serpent's head. To make an end of sin, of lawlessness, and the complete defeat of the author of sin—that is His work. But how is He to accomplish it?

We hear in our days much of civilization and the progress of civilization. A special phrase is "*our Christian civilization.*" The thought which has taken hold on multitudes in

Christendom is, that through Christ a great civilization is to be built up, which brings world improvement, a better world, and which will civilize heathen nations, who accept it. They think Christ in His teachings laid the foundation of a kingdom, a Christian era of continual progress, that through His principles the world is to become better and better, and gradually evil after evil is eliminated, the devil's power is curtailed, and finally this Christian civilization will end Satan's reign and will enthrone righteousness. And so they speak of "building the kingdom" which to the mind of millions of professing Christians is equivalent to a *progressive civilization*. As a result Christians, who according to the Word of God are not of this world, attempt in different ways to bring about certain results by legislation, by political measures and by new organizations. They finally conclude, as we hear it so much in our times, that the present world system is all wrong, capitalism must be dealt with, socialism, if not communism, are needed for this progressive civilization. Some speak of social Christianity. Then we see the attempts which are made to outlaw war, pacifism is advocated, in spite of the words of Christ who predicts the sword as well as wars and rumours of wars to the very end of this age.

Did Christ teach such a civilization, making the world better and better, gradually introducing righteousness and gradually conquering lawlessness? Where does He teach it? Only twisting and misapplying His words can uphold such a theory. *Christ did not come to civilize; He came to save.* We let another speak.

"If Christ's object had been to civilize the world, how easy it would have been for Him to have appeared on earth as the son of a Roman emperor (that need not have prevented His death on the cross)! As sovereign of the world He could have introduced a new era of Christian civilization and intellectual progress, with a perfect form of government, truly humane laws and abolition of slavery; an enlightened patronage of art and science; the promotion of trade, commerce, and industry. A few words would have revealed the knowledge of steam, electricity, and perhaps other

forces yet unknown. He could have solved all social problems; He could have put an end to all bodily suffering by some rational remedy, seconded by miraculous agencies and also given a constant supply of good products. All this lay in His power, "for whom are all things and by whom are all things" (Heb. ii:10). But how different from reality! Christ ignores completely the arts and sciences, the politics and legislation, and refuses to interfere even in a matter of right, with the words—"Man who made me a judge over you?" And when He stands before the representative of the most powerful empire of the world, instead of pointing out to him the enormous advantages of a civilizing Christianity, He answers briefly "My kingdom is not of this world."*

How true these words are! As stated before, all civilization aims at world improvement, at the gradual elimination of the curse; it is a process of evolution. It is like a man who is suffering from a terrible disease which has covered his whole body with boils and sores. The physician who comes to help him gives him a salve to apply. He treats the skin symptoms, but the source of the disease he never considers and never touches. Such is a boasted and progressive civilization. It is a delusion.

And has our civilization as it progressed during this age really brought true progress? Has it through the attempted obedience of the "golden rule" or the "principles of the sermon on the mount" produced more righteousness? Are the works of the devil through civilization, with its discoveries and inventions, getting less and less?

To any thoughtful mind it must surely appear that our age cannot boast of much progress. With and in spite of railroads, telegraph, telephone, the radio, moving pictures, television, rapid firing machine guns, torpedo boats, submarines, aerial navigation and a thousand other inventions and discoveries, wealth, contentment, peace and happiness have not come to mankind, nor have these things made

---

*Prof. Bettex, "Science and Christianity," page 210.

man more righteous and more law abiding. And the prospects of the future do not look better, but far worse.

In spite of boasted advance in government, in politics, in theology and jurisprudence, the tide of socialism and anarchy, as well as communism, is rising higher and higher, threatening to wipe out this boasted Christian civilization. Thrones and religions, all kinds of beliefs and laws, are being shaken, unemployment and crime increase, gangsters, kidnapers and all the rest of the underworld mock God and defy Him as well as man and his laws. Medical and educational sciences are continually recording new achievements, yet on all sides there is an increase of nerve and brain disorder; we hear of new diseases springing up which baffle medical science and in spite of higher education there is the growing insubordination and license of youth, and the frightful increase, in countries which boast of the highest type of civilization, of juvenile crime. Then for the last fifty years deadly instruments of warfare have been invented with poisonous gases and certain chemicals which inside of a few hours can destroy the earthly existence of tens of thousands of people. In one word, with all the inventions, the discoveries, the enlightenment, which are the leading characteristics of this age, lawlessness, crimes, discontent, unhappiness, national, international and individual, hatred, insanity and suicides are assuming alarming proportions. A *"Christian* Civilization?"

No Civilization is not the solution; it does not destroy the works of the devil, though some of this civilization may rest as a foundation on certain sayings of Christ.

The spot where God's triumph is achieved, God's Victory over sin, over lawlessness, is the Cross of Calvary, the Cross on which the Son of God died. In that Cross and *through the Cross the works of the devil were destroyed,* and the One who conquered him, is yet to bruise the serpent's head in the final triumph, as recorded in prophecy.

The highest expression of lawlessness, the greatest act of lawlessness was the rejection of Jesus Christ, the Son of God. The most lawless cry heard in history from human lips is the cry *"Away with Him! Crucify Him—Barabbas, the murderer, the serpent's seed is our choice—Away with Jesus"!*

That hour of lawlessness was the triumph of the serpent, when he used man to nail the Son of God to the Cross. But that hour, from which the holy Son of God shrank, in view of which His sweat became as great drops of blood, brought the serpent's defeat. The bruised heel is beginning to bruise his head.

How wonderful that God from His side uses the most lawless act committed in history to reveal through it His wisdom and His power! That Cross stood out in all eternity in God's purpose of redemption. It can never be forgotten in all eternity to come. In that cross, on which His holy Son, the Lord of glory, the Prince of Life died, God has provided the redemption for lost man and the ultimate regeneration of a marred creation. Here are the profoundest depths of wisdom, the greatest revelations of God in His righteousness and love, and here and here alone the way to God and Glory is revealed. And all so deep that we cry out, "O the depth of the riches both of the wisdom and knowledge of God! How unsearchable are His judgments, and His ways past finding out!" (Rom. xi:33).

Under the power of the serpent, instigated by the murderer from the beginning, man had delivered the Lord of glory to death. Was He, who had power over death, whose body knew no sin, helpless in the creature's hands? Could He have prevented the cruel death of the Cross? Is it true what the mob sneered at Him "He saved others, Himself He cannot save"? That was Satan's word. The truth is "Himself He *would* not save." When Peter arose to His defense with his sword, He said to him, "Thinkest thou that I cannot now pray to My Father, and He shall presently give Me more than twelve legions of angels? But how then shall the Scriptures be fulfilled, *that thus it must be*"? (Matt. xxvi:53, 54). He was not helpless. He could have escaped their hands and done what He had done so often before. Several times He used the significant phrase, "the hour is come." It was His hour, the hour ordained before the foundation of the world, when He was to carry out the will of God, the redemption of a ruined world. He was the willing victim and gave Himself to suffer and to die.

Yet all the cruelties and shame heaped upon Him were not sufficient to accomplish the work. He who knew no sin was to be made sin for us; man could not do that, God Himself had to do it. And so on that Cross the holy, spotless Son of God suffered in the place of guilty sinners from the righteous hand of God. God made Him sin for us. What that involved the finite mind can never understand. Depths are here which the creature can never measure; only the Godhead knows what it was when His holy soul was made an offering for sin, when He tasted death for everything.

The work is finished! God, through Christ and His work on the Cross, is victorious. The gulf which separates the holy Creator from His lost creature is bridged. The way back to God is now revealed and God in sovereign and infinite grace can deliver *"whosoever will,"* Jew or Gentile, from the guilt of sin, from the dominion of sin, from the law of sin and death, and restore forgiven sinners, not to an earthly Eden, but bring them as His beloved children, as the fellow-heirs of His Son, into the eternal fellowship with Himself in the Father's House above. Through His Son, God has won the victory over sin and lawlessness, over death, over the grave and the serpent's power.

And so God has given the Good News, the Gospel of His Son, in which He offers all the sinner needs. What is it?

Who can tell it out in its fullness? Man needs forgiveness, for He has sinned and by his works is an enemy of God. God in Christ offers a complete acquittal from all guilt, for Christ paid it all and made peace in the blood of the cross.

Man has a fallen sinful nature, the nature of flesh; it can do nothing else but sin; it is lawless. God offers a new nature, the gift of life, eternal life. Born again, with the new nature in him, man becomes a *new creation* in Christ Jesus, the old things (the old things of the old, the first

man) are passed away, all things are new. Man is under
the power and control of Satan; God has delivered him
from the power of darkness and translated him into the
kingdom of the Son of His love (Col. i:13). Man has no
strength, no power to do God's will and live in spiritual
harmony with Him, in His fellowship. God bestows the
power, an indwelling power through the gift of the Holy
Spirit, which enables man to walk in the Spirit and no
longer after the lusts of the flesh. Man is filled with fear
and uncertainty as to his destiny; God in the Gospel of
His Son delivers from the fear of death and the grave and
gives assurance that some day the redeemed shall be in
His presence, in unspeakable glory, forever with the Lord.
Such then is the glorious message of redemption, which
God has for the whole world. It is all His work of infinite
Love—for herein is Love; not that we loved God, but that
He loves us and gave His Son for a propitiation for our sins.
All can be obtained by acceptance of faith.

It is the greatest message God has for man, the message
for this present age. A greater message He cannot give.
It is a daring word to write, but it is true, in His redemption
offer in His Son, *God has exhausted His resources of Love
and Grace.* Through this message He is *not civilizing the
world,* but He is gathering all those who believe, into a
body, called the Church, the body and Bride of Christ.
This great purpose of this age will be accomplished. In
anticipation of what would take place during this age,
that the serpent would continue in the conflict, the Lord
Jesus Christ left the promise for His Church "*The Gates
of Hell (Hades) shall not prevail against it.*"

The prophecies of His physical resurrection were fulfilled
on the third day. He left the grave victorious over death,
so that His people can shout with Him "O, death, where
is thy sting? O grave where is thy victory?" Satan, the
serpent, would have rejoiced if that grave had been sealed
forever. He tried to keep Him there, that is the reason
his seed, the enemies of Christ, requested the Roman seal
and the guard. Satan is far ahead of the intelligence of

the modernistic scholars. He believes in prophecy; they do not. He knew that if Christ remained in that grave, He would be a defeated Christ and God would have failed. But in due time the victorious Christ ascended up on high and is now seated as the Head over all things at the right hand of God.

Before He left the earth He gave His commission to His own. What was it? Was it a commission to civilize the nations of the world, to abolish drunkenness by legislation, to outlaw war, to introduce socialism and communism, to bring in a new social order? Did He promise world conquest and a kingdom in which liberty, equality and fraternity are to rule? He left no such commission nor did He give such a promise. Before He departed He commanded, "That repentance and remission of sins should be preached in His Name among all nations, beginning in Jerusalem" (Luke xxiv:47). And again "Ye shall receive power, after that the Holy Spirit is come upon you and ye shall be witnesses unto Me both in Jerusalem, and in all Judea, and in Samaria, and unto the uttermost parts of the earth" (Acts i:8). That power came on the day of Pentecost with the gift of the Holy Spirit. What was the great witness given on that historic day? It was the witness to Christ and not a message to build a kingdom by which the nations become civilized and world improvement takes place. The great message of salvation was preached on that day, though not yet in all its blessed fulness. The result was the salvation of those who accepted it.

Before we follow the conflict, which continues throughout the present age, we mention in passing the record given in Acts i:41-47. Here we read that the Jews who had accepted Christ constituted a community. They sold their possessions and goods and had *all things in common*. Is not this a Christian Socialism?

Efforts have been made many times in the past to produce a Christian communism, but it always resulted in failure. The men who see here a program of world betterment through the socialistic idea do not go deep enough. They do not reckon with the fact that it was in Jerusalem this was done. It was an outward witness to the Jews that a great work had been done. In fact it was a witness to the Jews in Jerusalem that the crucified One is their Messiah, for such a blessed state of things is predicted to come when Messiah reigns. Some day it *will come* when Christ returns and His true kingdom will be established on earth. (See the question concerning that kingdom and Christ's answer in Acts i:6-7.) This socialism did not last long; it passed away as soon as Jerusalem had rejected the offer of the Gospel.

The first historic document of the new age, ushered in by the coming of the Holy Spirit, is the "Book of the Acts of the Apostles." In it we find the record of the activities of three supernatural persons—the risen Christ is spiritually with His own, as He had promised; then the Holy Spirit is here and acting in power. The third supernatural person is Satan, the old serpent. His oppositions are written large in this book. The one thing which displeased him the most and which stirred up his wrathful opposition is the preaching of Christ, His death and His resurrection. When Peter preached the second time and came to the statement "Unto you first God, having raised up His Son Jesus, sent Him to bless you, in turning every one of you away from your sins" (Acts iii:26) the enemy arose and Peter was arrested. The seed of the serpent, the unbelieving Jews, attempted to crush this testimony to Christ and when one arose, filled with the Holy Spirit, testifying to the fact that Jesus is standing at the right hand of God, the murderer from the beginning used the mob to kill Stephen (Acts vii). It was the signal for a great persecution. Satan thought his hour had come to end the testimony. The communistic society was forced to disband and was never reorganized. But as always "the wrath of the enemy must praise Him." The scattered company went everywhere preaching the great God-given message.

There was a greater victory than that. The leader of the persecution was one Saul of Tarsus. He was the instru-

ment of Satan to persecute the Church and to waste it.
Satan goaded him on to go as his agent beyond Israel's
land to continue his work of destruction. Then on the road
to Damascus the glory and power of the risen Christ laid
hold on him, as a brand snatched out of the fire. The
grace of God made him the mighty witness for Christ.
The chosen vessel with his testimony for Christ and the
Gospel of salvation became at once the object of the serpent's attack. The Jews took council to kill him. The
gates of Damascus were watched; he was smuggled out of
the city (Acts ix:23-25). Wherever he now carried the
fullness of that Gospel of a free, a full and a glorious salvation, he met the adversary. The serpent strikes at him.
He is scourged, beaten by the Jews, stoned and maligned.
Jews and Gentiles oppose him. He is arrested, in danger
of losing his life; new plots are concocted to kill him; he
suffers shipwreck and finally a deadly viper fastens itself
on his hand to attempt what the shipwreck had not been
able to do. The serpent is behind it all. Satan knew he
is heading for Rome to preach the Gospel there also "the
power of God unto salvation to every one that believeth."
He would prevent it; but he was defeated.

Let us suppose that the Apostle Paul instead of preaching
the message of the Cross, would have gone forth into the
heathen world with the idea of acknowledging the good
which is in the different pagan systems. Let us suppose
that he admired the classical literature of the Romans and
Greeks and their philosophies, appreciated their arts. Let
us suppose that he said—"we must acknowledge the good
traits in all these things" and instead of preaching Christ
and Him crucified, had used words of wisdom, excellency
of speech, which proved him an educated man, a liberal
man, thus gaining the respect of the heathen world. And
let us suppose when arriving in Rome he had suggested
different schemes by which certain moral evils in Rome,
drunkenness, prostitution, gambling, slavery and luxurious
living might be lessened or abolished. Would Satan have
opposed him? Would he have obstructed his path and

attempted his life? Certainly not! On the contrary he would have assisted in every possible way to help such a course, as long as the message of the Cross was ignored.

Let us not forget that the being who continues the conflict, attacking now the doctrine of Christ, the truth of Christ, the true Church of Christ, had also his agencies, those who belong to his seed. Besides the unbelieving Jews and Gentiles there was a Simon Magus, a child of the devil, doing his work (Acts viii); also Elymas the sorcerer, who had taken the name "Bar-Jesus" (Son Jesus); in Philippi a demon possessed damsel appeared to hinder the Gospel message (Acts xvi). He used the unseen evil spirits, which are at his command, in the mighty conflict.

And what happened in the beginning of the age continues throughout this age to the very end of it. Satan does not antagonize material progress; he is not alarmed at inventions and discoveries; he looks on with satisfaction when things become better outwardly in the world, when life becomes more liveable, by which the fact that curse rests upon all is almost forgotten; he can see idol temples crumble into dust to give way to another "religion," which may even have the prefix "Christian." He tolerates all this as long as the one great truth, the Cross, the salvation of God and its power, through the risen and living Christ, is pushed aside and not preached. He is willing to have great cathedrals put up, great institutions of learning for intellectual self-improvement founded, all kinds of societies and organizations formed, as long as the fact is not acknowledged or taught, that Christ, the seed of the woman, is the victorious Christ, who died for the sin of the world, the ever living One, through whom sin, lawlessness, the curse are to be destroyed.

Already in the apostolic age a tendency manifested itself to depart from the great redemption truths. Some denied the resurrection and an agnostic system denying the great pillars of the Gospel made itself felt. The Spirit of God warned that Satan transforms himself into an angel of light (2 Cor. xi:14), and to beware of the wiles of the devil. There is for true believers a warfare with the wicked spirits in the heavenly places (Eph. vi:11-14) and there are statements that doctrines of demons and teachings of seducing spirits are ready to corrupt (1 Tim. iv:1).

After the middle of the first century, a series of persecutions of Christians threatened the life of the church of Jesus Christ. They took place under different Roman emperors who were all of the serpent's seed. Through them Satan challenged the promise of Christ "that the gates of hell should not prevail against His Church." Thousands upon thousands, whom no historian has ever been able to compute, were cruelly tortured, crucified, burned alive and cast before wild beasts to be torn asunder and devoured. But instead of diminishing the Church, these persecutions increased the number of true believers. The blood of the martyrs became the seed of the Church and after several centuries, during which the enemy had done all he could to exterminate the church, Satan had to withdraw defeated.

This did not end the conflict for it continued in another form. As Satan corrupted the worship of Israel so he begins now to corrupt the doctrine of Christ and to introduce his deceptions and lies to defeat the purpose of God. The Cross and the blessed message of the Cross, the salvation of God, through faith in Him, who died as the Lamb of God, is what he continues to hate. He knows that through that message, if it is believed and accepted, God saves those who are the slaves of sin, and that these saved ones constitute the new man in Christ. He also knows well when finally God's purpose in this age is finished an.1 that mystical body of Christ is completed; that his dominion is over and his final defeat results.

The Lord Jesus had warned His disciples to beware of the leaven of the Pharisees and of the Sadducees and in connection with this He mentions their doctrine (Matt. xvi:11, 12). Note the order: Phariseeism first and Sadduceeism last. Phariseeism is ritualism, which teaches the traditions of men. Sadduceeism is rationalism, the denial of the supernatural, even as the Jewish Sadducees did not believe in angels or in the resurrection. Both, while our Lord was here, were His enemies and though they hated each other, finally Pharisees and Sadducees combined in the rejection of Christ. In the conflict of the present age this leaven is at work attempting the corruption of Christianity and the doctrine of Christ.

Ritualism displaces Christ as the only Saviour, denies His all-sufficiency, the efficacy of His blood, the sovereign grace of God, and sets aside His priesthood. Ritualism makes salvation dependent on works, on ecclesiastical membership, on the so-called "sacraments" and the ministrations of men.

Its rise dates back to the first century. There was already the tendency manifested in the assemblies in Galatia to listen to "another Gospel, which was not another," a counterfeit Gospel upon which not Paul, but the Holy Spirit, pronounced the curse (Gal. i:1-6). In that spurious teaching grace was set aside and the works of the law were declared needful for salvation and for righteousness. How solemnly true it is what the Holy Spirit dictated into the pen of Paul—"If righteousness come by the law, then Christ is dead in vain" (Gal. ii:21). In the days of aged John we find one Diotrephes, who did not give to Christ the preëminence, but loved to have the preëminence himself (3 John). He became a religious dictator, a forerunner of a domineering priesthood. And Peter, whom ritualism has put upon a pedestal of preëminence, which the fisherman of Galilee in true humility never claimed, warns teachers not to act as "lords over God's heritage."*

It was in the fourth century that the corruption of Christianity through ritualism and priestly assumption became prominent. The instrument was Constantine, misnamed, the Great. Many church historians have exalted him as one of the greatest benefactors of Christianity, when in reality he was a curse. We do not know if he saw the

---

*The word heritage is in the Greek " *Kleros*" from which is derived our English "Clergy." The unscriptural distinction between Laity and Clergy is here hinted at.

vision, which he claimed to have seen, a cross in the sky with the surrounding words "in this sign thou shalt conquer." The battle which was to decide his emperorship was won, and he carried out his vow that the Christian religion should become the religion of his empire. The Church and the world were then united and Christianity became a state-religion. It is true the cruel persecutions ended, but something worse took place. All the ritualistic inventions and superstitions have their beginning at this time. The peoples of the empire are now "made" Christians. They are forced by law and threat of punishment to drop their pagan customs. These are changed into "Christian" customs. Heathen days become Saints days; days nowhere commanded in the New Testament, like "Christmas" are introduced. Children are made Christians by "christening" them, that is by putting a little water on their heads. But the worst corruption came through the men who claimed to be priests and their audacious presumption.

Watch a snake in the grass! How it glides along nearer and nearer to its prey, till it makes the final dart to capture its victim. Thus the old serpent glided along in history, nearer and nearer the goal, to destroy the Gospel of Grace. Little by little error after error, perversion after perversion, corruption after corruption, are introduced. We have often been asked. When did the great ritualistic system known as the Romish Church originate? It is the product of growth, covering centuries. Look at some of the perversions! The worship of Mary and her adoration; the worship of saints, made by Rome and not by God; the worship of angels; pictures and statues become prominent and the knee is bowed before them; the inventions of a purgatory, and worse than all, the mass; holy water and the adoration of relics, the bones of saints and other objects: the invention of a sinful man becoming infallible as the vice-regent of Christ on earth, and a multitude of other things.

But where is Christ? Where is the message of God's Love and Grace? Where is the display of the power of God unto salvation and the realization of His eternal purpose?

It seemed as if Satan had defeated Christ after all. On account of the rejection of the true Gospel and the introduction of the lies of Satan, there came, as it always does with the denial of God's true redemption, a corresponding moral declension. The dark ages followed. A good part of the clergy became more and more corrupt, thieving, murdering and living in lust, committing crimes of every description. Some of the "vice-regents" developed into monsters. The crimes of the papacy are some of the worst in human history.

Yet in spite of all God's purpose is undefeated. Even during these dark ages He continues in His work through His Spirit. Not many, but some continue to preach the true doctrine of Christ and through their testimony new members are added to the body of Christ. And how many humble instruments the Lord must have had during the centuries of darkness whose names are not recorded in church history, but who are known in heaven?

During the fifteenth century the morning stars of the reformation begin to rise. The Spirit of God leads forward in restoring the forgotten truths of the work of Christ, by which the works of the devil will be destroyed. A Savonarola is heard with his fiery denunciations, for which he had to pay with his life. John Huss and others lift up their voices against the lies and wiles of the devil and the old serpent strikes at them and they fall as victims. Johannes Tauler and his friends with their godly teachings and efforts are harbingers of the coming change.

Finally, when the devil has over-reached himself in the vicious practices of the indulgences, selling forgiveness of sins beforehand, encouraging all crimes through the serpent's seed enthroned in Rome, the Spirit of God comes upon an obscure German monk. Martin Luther nails his ninety-five theses to the church door of Wittemberg.

He is used, having experienced himself salvation by grace, to herald once more the foundation truth of the Gospel, "the just shall live by faith." Other great men of God are raised up in other lands and endowed by the energy of the

Holy Spirit thunder forth the forgotten truths of the Gospel of Jesus Christ.

Like an angry poisonous serpent, knowing it is fighting for its life, the old serpent then began to hiss. The torture chambers of the satanic inquisition echo with the shrieks of countless thousands of men and women. The cruel murderer from the beginning almost exhausts his ingenuity in producing untold sufferings. The so-called "Christian" lands, Germany, France, England, Scotland, Ireland, the Netherlands, Bohemia, Italy, etc., are lit up by the horrible fires of the stakes and thousands perish. Whose work is it? The work of the murderer from the beginning! Once more he tries to defeat God by his acts of violence. Satan is defeated! The reformation sweeps on. In spite of tortures, dungeons and fires, God is victorious. What sufferings the old serpent produced! Let the history of the Waldensians, Spain, the Netherlands, the Huguenots and St. Bartholmew's Night give the answer. But all his ravenings could not defeat God. God continues in the execution of His purpose. The true Church is preserved.

Protestantism comes into existence next. It is far from bringing the full restoration of the truth and doctrine of Christ. It is true the great men used in this work were mighty men called by the Spirit of God. They were used in leading multitudes out of the old Roman sepulchre, where the Christ of God and the Gospel of Grace proclaimed through His finished work, had been buried so long. But some of the grave clothes remained. The teaching of sacramental powers, regeneration of infants through the application of water prevails. The simple memorial feast instituted in the night our Lord was betrayed, the breaking of bread and partaking of the cup, is still held by a good part of the Protestants as a ceremony of mystery and meritoriousness. Other erroneous doctrines are maintained. And certain vital truths are not preached, because unknown to the reformation. Soon conflicts arise. The reformation becomes involved in politics, becomes linked to the secular governments; the church becomes a state-church, a state institution, under the domination of princes, dukes, kings and emperors. Who does not recognize in these conflicts, upheavals and marring declensions, the work of Satan, the serpent!

The Lord Himself has given to us an estimate of Protestantism as it develops out of the reformation. In His message to Sardis, which prophetically refers to Protestantism,* He says: "I know thy works that thou hast a name, that thou livest, and art dead. . . . I have not found thy works perfect before God" (Rev. iii:1-2).

In the seventeenth and eighteenth centuries division arises also. Satan is in evidence everywhere as the perverter of the doctrine of Christ and the persecutor of those who preach the Gospel of His grace and who give a heroic testimony for Christ and sound doctrine.

With the eighteenth century there comes the rise of Sadduceeism. Rationalism now begins its leavening process, leavening, as it does in the twentieth century the whole lump.

To follow the history of rationalism would be impossible in a work like this. It is Satan's triumphant card through which he thinks he can win his game. *Rationalism is the way-preparer for the real end of the age,* the infidelity which ultimately brings about the revolt against God and against His Christ, leads to Atheism and the manifestation of the full mystery of lawlessness in the complete apostasy and its heading up in the man of sin, the final antichrist.

Rationalism starts with the rejection of the supernatural, and because the supernatural revelation is found in the Bible, the Word of God, it aims its destructive shafts first of all at the Book of books. Then follow denial upon

---

*We strongly advise our readers to study carefully and minutely the seven church epistles sent by the glorified Christ to the seven churches. Revelation II and III contain a divine forecast of the history of the Church on earth. *Ephesus* is the apostolic church going into declension; *Smyrna* is the Church persecuted; *Pergamos*, the Church being corrupted under Constantine; *Thyatira* is the Roman Catholic apostasy; *Sardis* presents the reformation period. *Philadelphia* and *Laodicea* describe the two leading currents of Protestantism.

denial. Christ is nothing but a religious leader, a teacher. His Saviourhood is denied altogether. Some even doubted His existence and spoke of Him as a myth.

Soon the fruits of rationalism appear. Every form of moral corruption follows. It was especially marked in England during the eighteenth century. But when it seemed as if all would be swept away and Satan through rationalism would destroy the Truth of God, God met the enemy in the great and marvelous revivals, which swept over Great Britain. The Wesleys and others, like Whitefield, were the leaders. Much of the existent rationalism was swept away like spiders' webs through the mighty energy of the Spirit of God. Thousands gathered everywhere to hear the great Gospel messages. Persecutions arose again, but Satan was unable to stem the rising tide which swept countless thousands into the kingdom. All classes of society were affected, the lowest and the highest wept penitential tears and found their refuge in the Cross of Christ. The revivals spread to the American colonies and elsewhere. As we show in a later chapter, this mighty work of the Spirit of God saved England from the terrible fate of France, one of the birthplaces of rationalism.

At the close of the eighteenth century Satan arose in his might and began his astounding activities in the conflict of the ages in which he aims at the destruction of governments, divine and human laws, the family and above all, the destruction of the Truth of God and the Church. The author believes that the demon-possessed Weishaupt with his *Illuminati* secret order, from which sprang the French revolution marks the beginning of the end of this age. The next chapters will follow more closely the workings of this mystery of lawlessness, which now in our own times is threatening to plunge the whole world into chaos and disaster.

It is written in Scripture: "When the enemy shall come in like a flood, the Spirit of the Lord shall lift up a standard against him" (Isa. lix:19). While the enemy made his preparations for the beginning of the final conflict, the

Holy Spirit also made His preparations. In the beginning of the nineteenth century long forgotten and obscured truths were recovered through the Spirit of God. Prophetic truths, so prominent in the beginning of the Church, were then brought to light and especially the midnight cry: "Behold, the Bridegroom cometh" was heralded. God's plan and purposes with Israel, their unfulfilled national promises, were also brought to light. Other truths like the character of the true Church as the Body and the Bride of Christ, the character of the present age and its end and related truths, are once more understood and preached.*

While Satan works towards the end of the age, the Spirit of God is also at work. As never before the true Gospel is preached everywhere. The recovery of the truth of the return of the Lord Jesus Christ to accomplish the crushing of the serpent's head, the promised consummation in the literal kingdom of Christ, led to the marvelous foreign missionary activities of the nineteenth century. The true Church realized as never before the commission of the soon coming Lord to preach the Gospel in the regions beyond and while Satan attempts over and over again the destruction of the Truth of God and the Church of God, the Gospel has its marvelous achievements in many lands and in the isles of the sea. Erstwhile cannibals become worshippers of God and countless thousands are added to the true Church called out from all nations. Explorers unlock the mysteries of interior Africa to be followed by the missionaries of the Cross. There was a constantly increasing triumph of the Gospel. In home lands revivals manifested the power of God unto salvation afresh, while the true children of God were drawn closer together and thus new expressions of the true unity of believers were brought about.

But as these mighty workings of the Spirit of God con-

---

*We have special reference to the mighty men of God, real scholars and at the same time humble men who were used in the recovery of these truths over a hundred years ago in the beginning of the movement known later by the name of "Plymouth Brethren." The most outstanding was John Nelson Darby.

tinued, the seed of the serpent under the direction of Satan, also developed an astonishing activity. The rise of socialism and anarchy is one of the leading features of the nineteenth century. The outcry against God and His Truth increased. As a result the revolutionary activities to end our civilization and to crush the Church became prominent. All this is described in our next chapter. Politically the groupings of nations in alliances, pacts and other combinations, one, the concert of Europe, took place. War follows war and everything becomes unsettled. Attempts to stop wars are made, but fail. Behind it all is the god of this age, who is ruling in sinister power. Nearer and nearer comes the goal of the political end of the times of the Gentiles as revealed in Daniel's prophecies.

Great things were expected with the dawn of the much lauded twentieth century. One third of it and more has passed into history. What has it brought forth? It would take an extra volume to give even a brief sketch of the rapid growth and development of the mystery of lawlessness. With the beginning of our century we see nations outdoing each other in building greater battleships, creating and supporting greater armies, calling millions of men into service, inventing new means for the wholesale destruction of human life. Torpedo boats, submarines, liquid fire, poisonous gases and scores of other inventions all are produced for the service of the murderer from the beginning. At the same time the unscriptural optimistic dreams of a misguided Christendom lead to all kinds of schemes to bring about universal peace. Instead of consulting the oracles of God and the revealed purpose of God in this age, the predictions as to its end, Christendom enters into politics. Preachers instead of preaching the one message God has ordained, turn pacifists and attempt various forms of reformation and world-betterment. The world must be made a decent place to live in. The evolution-delusion demands progress. Preaching the Gospel as commissioned by the head of the Church is too slow a process. Society has to be saved and war has to be outlawed.

Then comes the crash. Over night in 1914 the leading nations of Europe rush to arms and that at a time when religious leaders through political agitations thought that universal peace had been assured. The world war, the greatest tragedy in the history of our age, follows. A defeated Germany is the result and the map of Europe undergoes a change bringing out once more in the reconstruction the boundary lines of the Roman Empire. The political revival of that empire is next suggested and attempts are made to produce a united Europe in the United States of Europe. Jerusalem and Palestine are delivered and the dream of Zionism nears its realization. The wheat and the tares begin to ripen, and both are facing the predicted harvest in the end of the age. All corresponds to the infallible predictions of the Word of God. World preparations increase in leaps and bounds for the final conflict.

Satan, through rationalism, develops now greater opposition to God, His Son, and the doctrine of Christ. Destructive criticism is rampant. It invades all the different evangelical denominations and "Protestantism" is stripped of its power and former meaning. Universities, colleges, seminaries and similar institutions become permeated with the most dangerous infidelity true Christianity had ever faced before. It goes by the name of "modernism." It denies all the facts of the supernatural Christ and His work of redemption. The Blood of Jesus Christ, God's Son, which in God's sight is of an inestimable value, is rejected. Man no longer needs a Saviour, he is his own Saviour. The road leads further and further away from the revealed Truth of God, and a new paganism is fostered in the midst of Christendom. The road leads into the night of atheism.

Then appears the harvest of this rationalistic modernism. The Gospel of Christ, the power of God unto salvation, no longer believed is no longer preached. Modernistic leaders, who still cling to the evolution-delusion that the world must get better and better, turn to legislation and other political measures to bring improvement and curb crime. They find fault with existing government itself. They advocate a *"new social order"* and join hands with the ungodly elements and labor with them for a revolution, the annihilation of capitalism. What happens morally? The nation which boasts of being the leading nation of the world becomes the most lawless. Legislation put into the place of God's message, and that message rejected, brings an awful harvest. There follows an almost unbelievable increase of all crimes; a new trade appears in the form of "bootlegging"; the bootlegger is followed by the gangster, the gangster by the kidnaper. Thousands are murdered, yearly suicides increase at a frightful rate; every form of lawlessness increases. The corruption which is in the world through lust keeps also step with the acts of violence and lawlessness. A licentious literature is produced for the feeding of the flesh; amusements, the stage and the moving pictures become more vulgar, bordering on the obscene. Women dress in a shameless way. The females are emancipated and they show their liberty by blowing cigarette smoke into the faces of decent people.

The *"Christ-less reformers,"* who have no use for the Bible become the advocates of birth-control, companionate marriage, which is nothing less than legalized prostitution. Such is the harvest of rationalism, Satan's most powerful weapon against the Gospel of Jesus Christ.*

We do not forget the other side in this conflict. While Satan is marching on in his destructive work, God also is marching on. The modernistic denials have produced and are producing a new band of loyal witnesses. The Spirit of God stirs them by His power to contend earnestly for the faith. As a result a separation takes place. The true believers are drawn closer together; unscriptural denominational lines are abandoned. In the different denominations the conflict rages. As far as the conservatives are concerned, who hold fast His Word and do not deny His Name,

---

*Another work of Satan is delusionism in systems like Christian Science, Unity, New Thought, Theosophy, Spiritism, Occultism, Mental and Faith Healing cults, etc.

it is a losing battle. They are defeated in assemblies and great church gatherings. Modernism is forging ahead, in its blind unbelief rushing onward to its appointed end. Yet in spite of it all the Spirit of God continues His mighty work. Satan cannot silence the preaching of the Gospel; its blessed sound is heard everywhere and thousands are still added to the body of Christ. God's purpose is rapidly being accomplished. In Russia, where the powers of darkness are trying to crush out the Church and the truth of God through the society of the godless, hundreds are saved everywhere and added to the Church, the body of Christ. It is a repetition of former persecutions. The true Church prospers. Like the burning bush, which Moses saw, the fires burn, but the bush is not consumed.

In concluding this chapter we point to one of the most startling facts relating to these modern conditions in Christendom and the apparent success of the powers of darkness. Rationalistic modernism makes audacious claims, boasting that the destruction of the dogma, that is supernatural Christianity, is in sight. In this respect the liberals are on the same footing with free-thinkers and atheists. They also in their blindness see the overthrow of true Christianity. The great mass of Christians who labor under the unscriptural conception that this age must be getting better, that the world must be gradually converted to God and that "His kingdom" is to be built up, in the midst of the increasing denials and the resultant corruption and moral bankruptcy, are greatly bewildered.

But here is the startling fact: all we see now in the political, the religious, the social and commercial world is prewritten in the Word of God. The age will end and must end. We see the end is here. The age does not set in a glorious evening sky, but the sky is red and lowering; foul weather is approaching—that is the prophetic testimony of the New Testament. The political end of this age is fully revealed in the prophecies of Daniel, which we do not follow here.*

*The author's exposition of Daniel has helped thousands in understanding these prophecies. (225 pages, 85 cents postpaid).

Our Lord did not hold out the false hope of world improvement or world conversion in His great prophetic Olivet discourse (Matt. xxiv-xxv). He announced beforehand the events which should take place, and every one has come to pass. He tells us that the age will be capped by a "great tribulation" a time of world trouble.

The testimony of the Holy Spirit through the writers of the New Testament—Paul, Peter, John, James and Jude gives a still greater line of predictions as to the age-ending. The rationalism, the leaven of the Sadducees, and its work in corruption during this age, and especially at its close, is minutely revealed. Let us listen to some.

"Now the Spirit speaketh expressly, that in the latter times (the end of the age) some shall depart from the faith, giving heed to seducing spirits and the doctrines of demons" (1 Tim. iv:1).

"This know also, that in the last days perilous times shall come. For men shall be lovers of their own selves, coveteous, boasters, proud, blasphemers, disobedient to parents, unthankful, unholy, without natural affection, truce breakers, false accusers, incontinent, fierce, despisers of those that are good, traitors, heady, high-minded, lovers of pleasure more than lovers of God. Having a form of godliness, but denying the power thereof; from such turn away" (2 Tim. iii:1-5).

"The time will come when they will not endure sound doctrine; but after their own lusts shall they heap to themselves teachers, having itching ears; and they shall turn away their ears from the truth, and shall be turned to fables" (2 Tim. iv:3, 4).

"But there were false prophets also among the people, even as there shall be false teachers among you, who privily shall bring in damnable heresies, even denying the Lord that bought them, and bring upon themselves swift destruction. And many shall follow their pernicious ways by reason of whom the way of truth shall be evil spoken of" (2 Peter ii:1-2).

"There shall come in the last days scoffers, walking after their own lusts, and saying, 'Where is the promise of His coming?'" (2 Peter iii:3, 4).

"Little children, it is the last time, and as ye have heard that antichrist shall come even now there are many antichrists, whereby we know that it is the last time * * * he is antichrist, that denieth the Father and the Son" (Just what modernism is doing) (1 John ii:18, 22).

"Certain men * * * denying the only Lord God, and our Lord Jesus Christ" (Jude iv).

"Go to now, rich men, weep, howl for your miseries that shall come upon you * * * ye have heaped treasures together for the last days * * * behold the hire of the labourers who have reaped down your fields, which is of you kept back by fraud crieth; and the cries of them which reaped are entered into the ears of the Lord Sabaoth" (James v:1-7).

The final end of the age in apostasy, under the reign of the lawless one, the man of sin, the final antichrist, is more fully revealed in the Second Epistle to the Thessalonians. The seventh chapter will deal with the future consummation of the mystery of lawlessness, the final conflict and the defeat of the serpent, in the light of this passage (2 Thess. ii).

CHAPTER V

The Modern Origin and Development of the Forces of Lawlessness

We have traced the great conflict between darkness and light, between truth and error, between righteousness and unrighteousness in a general way. To understand the more modern source of the serpent-controlled powers which now aim at world revolution, the dethronement of righteousness and truth, the establishment of what is called "a new world order," we must go for a starting point to the eighteenth century. It was during the last half of that century of disaster that a secret order, known by the name "*Illuminati*," came into existence. A similar movement, known also as "Satanism" had existed before. Already in 1185 a secret order had functioned under the name "*Confrérie de la Paix*," the brotherhood of peace. It was a pacifist attempt to make an end of all wars. They had the communistic idea of bringing about ownership of all lands by the people. Besides attacking all rulers they hated the Church and attempted the destruction of castles, monasteries and churches. It was one of the earlier attempts of a godless Communism.

Early in the eighteenth century a set of French infidel and immoral philosophers began to spread their anti-christian and anti-civilization teachings. A notable one was the notorious J. J. Rosseau. Most of his theories contain the pernicious germs of socialism and communism. He expressed hatred of all civilization, which, in his opinion, was all wrong. He went so far as to say that civilization is the curse of humanity, that under restraint man had been robbed of his liberty and that the prevailing laws of property were responsible for the misery of the people. He advocated a return to primitive conditions. In his writings may be traced the shouts of the French Revolutionists—"Liberty—Equality—Fraternity." Certain secret lodges of France, through which later the revolution was supported, used the same words.

But it remained for a German to exploit the suggestions of Rousseau and to become the inventor of a system which is now fully carried out by Sovietism. It marks the beginning of the final great battle of the conflict of the ages.

Adam Weishaupt, one of the most prominent "seeds of the serpent" was born in 1748 in Bavaria. As a young man he turned to the works of these French Philosophers and also dabbled in occultism, through which he probably yielded himself to the powers of darkness. Certain forms of a vicious occultism, a veritable Satanism, devil worship and the black mass, were then practised. He re-stated Rousseau's delusion.

"Man is fallen," he said, "from the condition of liberty and equality, the state of pure nature. He is under subordination and civil bondage arising from the vices of man." Then, serpent-like, he struck at religion. "Man is not bad except as he is made so by arbitrary morality. He is bad because religion, the state, and bad example pervert him." And so he said, that from the mind of man there must be rooted out the belief in a life after death and the fear of any future judgment. *Reason* must become the religion of man and when that happens the problem will be solved. He attacked the family and national life; he hated patriotism. All social ties must be dissolved. He followed closely in the steps of the immoral Rousseau. "It was not, however, in his diatribes against civilization that Weishaupt surpassed Rousseau, but in the plan he devised for overthrowing it. Rousseau had merely paved the way for revolution, Weishaupt constructed the actual machinery of revolution itself."*

On the first day of May, 1776, the year in which our beloved country, the American Republic, was born, Weishaupt founded with a number of adherents a secret society, patterned after French freemasonry, which he called "*Illuminati.*" All members were required to adopt other names.

---

*World Revolution," by Mrs. Nesta Webster, page 8. Mrs. Webster's book is a most reliable historical work. It is unfortunate that this valuable work is out of print.

We shall see later how the Jewish leaders of the Russian revolution also changed their names, following the example of the original Illuminati. The members of the Illuminati lodges were instructed to maintain the strictest secrecy as to the proposed world-revolution and to hide their antagonism to religion. They claimed that Christ Himself was the author of Illuminism. New candidates were told: "That no one paved so sure a way for liberty as our grand master Jesus of Nazareth, and as Christ exhorted his disciples to despise riches, it was in order to prepare the world for that community of goods that should do away with property." So subtle were their methods that many Protestant preachers, misguided as they were, fell in with the *Illuminati*, and accepted the belief that Illuminism was a practical expression of Christianity. It is not different today, for in the ranks of socialism and communism we find many clergymen of different denominations, who blindly, and blinded by the god of this age, think that these subversive movements will help the advancement of the "kingdom" among men, a term which in its Biblical meaning is wholly misunderstood by them.

In 1777 Weishaupt joined the freemasons and a closer alliance of Illuminism with Freemasonry was brought about. After that a congress at Wilhelmsbad was held and there a great conspiracy against monarchy and the church was hatched out. At the same time Jews came into prominence who were no longer excluded from the illuminized lodges. Fortunately there arose dissensions among the leaders of Illuminism, on account of the increasing tyranny of Weishaupt. The dissatisfied members, among them four college professors, appeared before a court of inquiry. The evidences they furnished left no further room for doubt as to the devilish nature of Illuminism. It was shown that the plan aimed at the destruction of all governments and all religions. They had adjured Christianity and advocated sensual pleasures, having brought into their membership prostitutes. Death they declared was nothing but "eternal sleep." The best information of all this may be gained by a volume, now quiet rare, by a contemporary writer, Mr. Robison.*

According to his investigation the Illuminati "accounted princes and all rulers usurpers and tyrants; patriotism was denounced; they would endeavor to abolish all laws which protected property. They intended to establish universal liberty and equality, to root out all religion and ordinary morality and to destroy the bonds of domestic life by doing away with marriage and by taking the education of children out of the hands of the parents." The aims of the Illuminati were grouped around six points: (1) The Abolition of Monarchy and all other governments; (2) The Abolition of private property; (3) The Abolition of Inheritance; (4) The Abolition of Patriotism; (5) The Abolition of the family life, of marriage and the communal education of the children; (6) The Abolition of all religion. This six-pointed program of abolition is now functioning in Russia through Communism and its ever-spreading propaganda. Behind it stands the unseen power of darkness.

Finally the authorities acted in 1786. The secret papers of the Illuminati were seized and revealed beyond the shadow of a doubt the damnable and diabolical conspiracy of world-revolution. Weishaupt with a price set upon his head, became a fugitive. Then the Illuminati spread the lying report that they had disbanded. It was not the truth; they continued their agitations with greater secrecy. Illuminism became the most powerful leaven in all the European countries; it is working in the twentieth century towards its fatal goal as never before.

There is no question at all in the minds of historians that Illuminism was responsible for the French revolution. Much of the reign of terror emanated from the Jacobin Club, which originated in 1789 and was organized by certain disciples of Weishaupt, among them Robespierre and Mirabeau. The Jew Cagliostro, who played an important part, was also an Illuminatus. We cannot follow the terrible story of the French revolution in detail. All the

*Robison, "Conspiracy of World Revolution," 1793.

Satanic plans of the Illuminati, even to the enlisting of immoral women, were literally carried out. The watchword of the lodges of the Illuminati became the slogan of the revolution—"Liberty; Equality; Fraternity." Then a proclamation was issued summoning the proletariat of all Europe to rise in revolt against all ordered governments, but it proved a failure. In 1793 the abolition of religion was carried out. Some time before all over France the priests were murdered. The feasts of reason were established and prostitutes were enthroned as goddesses. The entire abolition doctrine of Illuminism permeated the revolution. The phrase "sovereignty of the people" was coined and from that time on history records the "rising of the people," the so-called proletariat. The reign of terror was the partial harvest of Illuminism. One of the most awful attempts, only partly carried out, was the depopulation of France on a large scale. Kill them off by the millions— the bourgeoisie! But according to the best statistics the many millions of victims, as boasted, did not fall in the French revolution. How insignificant it is in comparison with the millions which were murdered by the Bolsheviki in the second Russian revolution! When it was all over in France, France was demoralized, impoverished, exhausted and wretched beyond description.

Then came the conspiracy of another Frenchman, Babeuf, in 1796. He formed a secret Directorate fashioned after the Illuminati order. As Weishaupt had surrounded himself with twelve disciples so Babeuf selected twelve confidants. A great manifesto was prepared by him. It began with the announcement—"For fifteen hundred years you have lived in slavery and consequently in unhappiness." He promised, as Weishaupt had done, "The community of goods" and repeated the Illuminati statement: "The goods of the earth belong to every one." The manifesto also contained a very significant statement. "The French revolution is only the forerunner of another revolution, very much greater, very much more solemn, which will be the last." He spoke as a Satan-inspired prophet. Over a hundred years later the very much greater revolution passed into history in Russia. A contemporary writer, Edouard Fleury, has given in his work an analysis of his doctrines. It is most astonishing to find them perfectly reproduced in the present day Communism. His aim was the establishment of the "Republic of the Equals." Community of goods and labor was to be enforced. Children were to be given over at their birth to the state and trained in institutions. Family relations and family life were to be abolished entirely. How the greater revolution has followed this pernicious path we shall find later.

Finally Babeuf announced a "great day of the people" when all should be carried out with the wholesale slaughter of the wealthy, the bourgeoisie and all in authority. All France was to run with rivers of blood. One man by name of Grisel had been drawn against his will into the conspiracy. Providence in a most remarkable way used him to uncover the hellish plot. The police raided the headquarters of the conspirators and found Babeuf and his right hand man Buonarotti working on the posters calling the people to revolt. All the leaders were cast into prison and dealt with by the law; Babeuf and others with him were executed. But his system was far from being dead. The Russian revolution accomplished what Babeuf had planned.

Vicious Illuminism was spreading in every direction and appeared in all countries of Europe. Amongst those won over we find Thomas Paine. In his book, "The Age of Reason," he betrays his Illuminati fellowship. In 1786 Illuminism made its appearance in Virginia and an attempt was made to circulate in a secret way the Illuminati doctrines. The exposure given in the work of Robison and others opened the eyes of statesmen and preachers. They raised a warning cry. Reverend Jedediah Morse of Charlestown preached his great sermon on May 9, 1798 on Illuminism, in which he said:

"Practically all of the civil and ecclesiastical establishments in Europe have already been shaken to their foundations by this terrible organization; the French Revolution itself is doubtless to be traced to its machinations; the success of the French armies are to be explained on the same grounds. The Jacobins are nothing more or less than the open manifestation of the hidden system of the Illuminati. The order has its branches established and its emissaries at work in America. The affiliated Jacobin Societies in America have doubtless had as the object of their establishment the propagation of the principles of the illuminated mother club in France."*

His text was "This is a day of trouble and of rebuke and blasphemy." Needless to say the warnings by godly, Bible-believing and Gospel-preaching preachers were heeded. And today—what a change! We have in American pulpits hundreds of men who have cast the messages of the Bible to the winds, who preach Socialism and call themselves "The Friends of the Soviets." They are the sickly looking "Pinks" and with their boasted friendship for Russia they endorse the program of destruction.

Let us listen to the President of Yale in New Haven in 1798, Dr. Timothy Dwight. He preached a sermon the same year in which he spoke of the Illuminati French revolution:

"No personal or national interest of man has been uninvaded; no impious sentiment of action against God has been spared; no malignant hostility against Christ and His religion has been unattempted. Justice, truth, kindness, piety, and moral obligation universally have not merely been trodden under foot but ridiculed, spurned, and insulted as the childish bugbears of drivelling idiocy . . . For what end shall we be connected with men of whom this is the character and conduct? It is that our churches may become temples of reason, our Sabbath a decade, and our psalms of praise Marseillaise hymns? Is it that we may see the Bible cast into a bonfire, the vessels of the sacramental supper borne by an ass in public procession, and our children either wheedled or terrified, uniting in the mob, chanting mockeries against God, and hailing in the sounds of the 'Ca ira' the ruin of their religion and the loss of their souls? Shall our sons become the disciples of Voltaire and the dragoons of Marat, or our daughters the concubines of the Illuminati?"†

And today—what a change! Many of our colleges and universities have for professors, Atheistic evolutionists, who

---

*Quoted in "World Revolution," page 79.
†Ibid., page 79-80.

exhibit a malignant hostility to Christ and everything supernatural, who have trodden underfoot all divine truth, who are the outspoken advocates of Socialism, Communism and world revolution. *What a change!*

After the collapse of the French revolution the development of the mystery of lawlessness continued with its antagonism to God and Christ and all law and order. When Napoleon came into power, during the fifteen years of his regime Illuminism was cowed and its vicious propaganda was arrested. But like a smothered fire breaking out afresh when winds fan the smouldering embers, so Illuminism flared up with new energy. The revival took place in Germany. One of the leaders of the French revolution was a German, Baron Anarchasis Clootz. This Prussian was an Illuminatus, a follower of Weishaupt and a rabid enemy of Christianity. He was the coiner of the word "Septemberize," because in September, 1792, a large number of French priests and religious leaders had been murdered. Clootz regretted that all religious leaders had not been "Septemberized." He declared many times that he is "the personal enemy of Jesus Christ." When in 1812 the *"Tugendbund"* (a misleading name—the bond of virtue) was organized, the Illuminati doctrines and the perversions of Clootz were found to be underneath it, as well as underneath the many secret societies, which continued the slogan of the Illuminati and the Revolution: "Liberty; Equality; Fraternity." The anti-Christian movements pread to Italy and to other countries and increasingly the Jews took a leading role in the program of revolution.

In England, Socialism made its first appearance through a wealthy mill owner, Robert Owen. For a time he was the benefactor of the people. He established the industrial system on a new basis and attempted a co-operative movement. He had a model shop in which all goods were sold to the people at cost price. His experiment became very popular and successful, but unfortunately the good which his philanthropic schemes were doing was finally completely destroyed by Owen becoming an out and out Illuminatus.

He echoed all the vicious abolitions of Weishaupt and branded the existing society all wrong, advocating vigorously the annihilation of all civilization. As to his character, he was a riddle. For years he was a professing Christian, bent on doing good to his fellowmen, but when he adopted Illuminism he became anti-Christian. This erratic Socialist finally attempted colonization on Communistic lines in America. He bought a large tract of land called "Harmony" from the followers of one Pastor Rapp. He named it "New Harmony Colony of Equality." It proved a great failure in the end.

Another leader on continental Europe was Saint Simon, who followed the theories of Babeuf and therefore advocated strongly the destruction of civilization. But he went at it in a most subtle way. He claimed he was but following the teachings of Christ, just as the American religious modernists do, the friends of the Soviets. He asserted that his system was simply aiming at the fulfilment of the teachings of Christ as to the brotherhood of man. A few years later he exemplified his teachings by trying to blow out his brains.

After Saint Simonism had collapsed, Fournier, Buchez, Louis Blanc, Cabet and others took up the serpent's work. Cabet attempted colonization in America. He had colonies in 1847 in Texas, later in the old Mormon town of Nauvoo, Illinois. But as he himself developed into a Communistic autocrat, a revolt took place and his schemes ended in complete failure. Then followed a veritable horde of theorists advocating different forms of socialism and communism.

One of the new theories invented in 1836 dealt with the socialization of industries, banks, mines, and the newly invented means of transportation. A hundred years later in the Spring of 1933 a certain Methodist Conference under the leadership of a socialistic Bishop received a resolution advocating "that the people of the United States be made owners of the natural resources, such as coal, iron, oil and water-generated electricity, and of our banking institutions, railroads, steel, cotton and woolen mills. Inflation, the lowering of trade barriers, the adjustment of war debts now being set forth as possible solutions of the depression are not genuine cures for the sickness of our capitalistic society." Another religious body suggested as a cure of conditions "the equal distribution of wealth."*

Next appeared Anarchy as a system. It was brought about through Prudhon, who declared that no government had any right to exist. It is somewhat different from communism. Communism wants all lands, wealth and property taken out of the hands of private owners and be given over to the State, as it has been done in Russia. Anarchy aims at the destruction of the State and advocates the seizure of everything by the people. Prudhon, the father of Anarchism, was a terrible blasphemer, following the vicious Illuminati, Weishaupt, Babeuf, Clootz and the others. He said—"God is cowardice, folly, tyranny, evil and misery. For me then, *Lucifer, Satan.*" He became associated with a Russian, Bakunin, who took a leading part in the development of the mystery of lawlessness through the power of Satan.

Born in 1814 he belonged to the Russian nobility. He was an incorrigible youth, living on other people's money and finally took up a career, which like many others, including Karl Marx, he found both easy and remunerative, the career of a revolutionist. He became the tool of the shrewd German Jew, Marx, who used him for a certain time. He took a leading part in the revolutions of 1848 in Russia, Prague and in Saxony, where he was arrested. He was turned over to Russia and kept in prison for a number of years and finally sent to Siberia. He escaped and reached London via Japan and America. He then continued his vicious propaganda. His favorite toast was "To the destruction of all law and order and the unchaining of all evil passions."

As a disciple of Weishaupt he found a man of kindred mind in Netchaieff. They organized the "*International*

*"Our Hope," July, 1933.

Alliance of Social Democracy," which followed closely the Illuminati doctrine. Here is Bakunin's declaration:

"The Alliance professes atheism. It aims at the abolition of religious service, the replacement of belief by knowledge and by human justice, the abolition of marriage. Above all, it aims at the definite and complete abolition of all classes and the political, economic, and social equality of the individual of either sex. The abolition of inheritance. All children to be brought up on a uniform system. It aims directly at the triumph of the cause of labor over capital. It repudiates so-called patriotism and the rivalry of nations and desires the universal association of all local associations by means of freedom.

"The final aim of this society is 'to accelerate the universal revolution'."

His associate Netchaieff was a ferocious fellow. Night and day he had but one thought—relentless destruction. He despised any kind of reform movements and said: "Every effort is to be made to heighten and increase the evil and the sorrows which will at length wear out the patience of the people and encourage mass insurrection. A series of monstrous acts will drive the people to revolt."

It is next to impossible to trace historically the ever-increasing growth of the revolutionary movements, the intrigues and viciousness of their leaders and how the two groups represented by Marx, the Jew and the Russian Bakunin, clashed. Both had prominent parts in the different revolutions. It came finally to a break in the Spring of 1871. Marx and his fellow Jews, Nicholas Outine, Hess, Liebknecht, Bebel and other German Jews tried to expel Bakunin from the Internationale held in 1864. A long struggle followed, Netchaieff was exposed as a fraud and Marx as a liar. Some of the deceptions practised are almost unbelievable. Finally the Bakuninists were expelled and Marx terminated the first Internationale.

Karl Marx had appeared as one of the most prominent Jewish leaders of the revolutionary activity. He was the son of a Jewish lawyer, by name of Mordecai. He was born in 1818 and went in his youth to Paris to study, but was soon expelled from France on account of his revolutionary propaganda. Marx had found a suitable associate in Friedrich Engels with whom he organized the Communist League. A year before the revolution of 1848 he issued his *"Communist Manifesto,"* the celebrated document which Socialism and Communism have spread throughout the world. Here is the final paragraph:

"Communists scorn to hide their views and aims. They openly declare that their purpose can only be achieved by the forcible overthrow of the whole extant social order. Let the ruling classes tremble at the prospect of a communist revolution. Proletarians have nothing to lose but their chains. They have a world to win. Proletarians of the world unite."

The Manifesto of this Jewish-Atheist, an impostor, as it has been proved, is the basis of the attempted world revolution of our times. During the revolution of 1848 he headed the Communistic Society in Berlin, which was responsible for many murders. He was arrested, found guilty and condemned to death but escaped to England. There he wrote the book, which Communists call their "Bible," that is "Das Kapital" (Capital). It is a very poorly written and obscure work. His Manifesto was heralded as the charter of freedom of the workers of the world. Even a superficial reading shows that it is Illuminism pure and simple—the same abolitions are urged and the community of women is advocated. If Marx did not study the writings and theories of Weishaupt, Babeuf, Blanc, Clootz, Cabet and many others, and as a plagiarist reproduced them in a work he palmed off as his own, then an evil power must have guided his hand when he wrote his Manifesto. But it is a proven fact that he spent many months in the British Museum where he had access to the revolutionary literature from which he constructed his theories, fraudulently claiming they were his own. We quote from "World Revolution":

"He collected all the materials for his book in the reading room of the British Museum. It was there he found his whole system ready to hand. Can we not see him, like some veteran Jewish rag-and-bone merchant, going over the accumulated debris of past social schemes, passing through his fingers the dry bones of dead philosophies, the shreds and tatters of worn out doctrines, the dust and ashes of exploded theories, and with the practical cunning of the German and Hebrew brain shrewdly recognizing the use that might be made of all this lumber by skilfully welding it into one subversive whole? Marx was an impostor from the beginning. Posing as the Prophet of a new Gospel, he was in reality nothing but a plagiarist without the common honesty to pay tribute to the sources whence he drew his material."*

He raved like a madman against Capital and Capitalistic systems, and now the harvest of the seed sown by this demonized man is ripening throughout the world. The terrible aspect of it is that hundreds of religious leaders and educators of Gentile Christendom have become so blinded that they have abandoned the true Gospel of Jesus Christ, the power of God unto salvation, and, after giving up the faith supernaturally given to man in the Bible, turn to Socialism, as Dr. Sherwood Eddy has done and a horde of others, raising an outcry against Capitalism. Thus these men, who still use the word "Christian" are siding with the Marxian reproduction of the satanic Illuminism, and in this way become associated with the evil forces which constitute the mystery of lawlessness.

And Marx, with all his denunciation of capitalism and his frantic appeals to the workers of the world to arise, was a miserable hypocrite who lived on the capital made in the exploitation of the workers. He lived in luxuries through the wealth which his associate had accumulated, grinding it out of the poor workingmen. Friedrich Engels, his associate, who lacked in the brains and cunning of Marx, had made a large fortune in a Lancashire cotton spinning mill. Marx never worked, but lived on Engel's money. We quote once more "World Revolution":

"We have the ludicrous situation of these two German (Jewish) opponents of Capitalism and industrial exploitation living complacently on capital accumulated from the exploitation of English workers! How in the face of this fact can any one retain a lingering belief in the genuineness of Marx's Socialism? Indeed the more we study Marx's writings—not those intended for publication, but the real expressions of his opinions contained in his private correspondence the more the conviction is borne in upon our minds that Marx never believed a word of the doctrines he professed, but that to him Socialism was merely a system to be made use of for his own ends."†

*"World Revolution," page 170.
†"World Revolution," page 172.

This is true of other Socialistic, Communistic leaders. They are the greatest exploiters of the proletariat, the workers, whom they enslave with a worse slavery than the supposed slavery of capitalism. The author read recently a volume written by one of the former associates of Lenin, Krassin, Litvinoff and others.* He repented of his association and in his volume uncovers the selfishness and the frauds of these Soviet leaders. Such are your leaders, ye modernistic Socialists, ye Communistic Pinks!

French Socialism had been weakened and as it passed away with the revolution of 1848 the German Social Democracy took its place under an atheistic leadership, the leadership of Lassale, Marx, Engels and others.

As we are writing not a history of Socialism, but are tracing briefly the development of the different forms of the mystery of lawlessness from its inception in the previous century we must pass over the events of the great revolutionary year 1848 which, for a time, held all Europe in its grasp. The stolen theories of Marx, a revival of Illuminism in a new garb, took hold everywhere. "Let the ruling class tremble at the prospect of a Communist World Revolution," Marx had said and such a world revolution against governments, patriotism, private ownership, the family, all law and order and especially against God and against Christ loomed up larger and larger on the political horizon of the second half of the nineteenth century.

In 1864 the first Internationale was held. It was held in London and was based entirely upon the Communist Manifesto of Marx. Outwardly he had little to do with it, yet he was the unseen power behind this first attempt to carry out his call: "Workers of the World Unite!" The great demand made was "the abolition of every kind of class domination." In this Internationale anti-christianity became very prominent. It was supported by certain lodges which merged into *"The International Association of Working Men."*

*G. Solomon *"Unter den Roten Machthabern"*—Under the Red Autocrats.

The subsequent congresses held in affiliation with the Internationale, especially the Student Conventions, demonstrated the hatred of the unseen backer of the movement, Satan. In Liege, France, such a congress declared:

"What we wish for, we revolutionaries and socialists, is physical, moral, and intellectual development of the human race. Note that I say physical first, intellectual afterwards. We wish, in the moral order, by the annihilation of all prejudices of Religion and the Church, to arrive at the negation of God."

And a similar Congress held in Brussels ended with the cry—"War on God! Hatred towards God! That is our Progress!"

As already stated, the first Internationale terminated on account of the clash between the Socialistic-Communistic views of Marx and the Anarchism of Bakunin. The "International Association of Working Men" held a number of conventions in which the program of destruction, of murder and all that goes with it was upheld. So horrible were the intrigues, the frauds connected with it, besides the attempts at world revolution, that honest Socialists turned away with disgust from these demon-possessed leaders. A prominent socialist, Fribourg, wrote: "I insist that it should be known, that no upright mind could have conceived the idea of giving birth to a society of war and hatred."

Then came the revolution of 1871. Germany had won her great victory over France. Bismarck in power had accomplished a program of Pan-Germanism. In connection with it all the perfidy of Marx came to light. He became a faithful servant, for his own selfish end, of German Imperialism. He was denounced as a secret agent of Bismarck and accused of having accepted a large sum of money from him. All these facts are substantiated by the private correspondence of the impostor. Both Marx and Engels, as German patriots, applauded the victories of the German armies and revealed their treacheries towards the Internationale by trying to persuade the French Proletariat not to fight the German invaders. It was the defeat of

the French which gave birth to the revolution in France.
Bakunin, now the opponent of Marx, was prominent in it.
When the Prussians entered Paris the revolution broke
out in all its fury. The revolutionaries, carrying the red
flag became masters of Paris; it was anarchistic and as a
result the commune was formed. Horrible scenes were
enacted again in this revolution, charged mostly to foreigners
who had been brought to France for that purpose. Hatred
against God and Christianity broke out afresh. Churches
were desecrated. Illuminism, this Satan-begotten system,
was evident throughout this revolution. But again the
forces of law and order were victorious, after nearly fifty
thousand people had been killed.

We have to go next to Russia to find an expression of
the working of the mystery of lawlessness under the name
of *Nihilism.* A French writer in the beginning of the
nineteenth century, Joseph de Maistre, had termed the
Illuminati "Rienistes."* The nihilists were the same
anarchistic revolutionists. The leader was a Russian,
Prince Koropotkine, born in 1842. Nihilism, besides advocating the overthrow of governments, demanded the equality
of sexes, aiming at the destruction of the family and the
sanction of free love. Above all, all religions must be
abolished; they were the sworn enemies of the Church.
That there were serious causes for revolution in Russia
under the autocracy of the Czars is most true. Alexander
II had begun a splendid era of reform. The emancipation
of the serfs had taken place in 1861, but no reform, no promise of better things in any way curtailed the nihilistic
agitation. They were out for a demolition of civilization,
the abolition of government and religion. When the
Russian government fought the nihilist, they began a
series of assassinations. The most prominent was the
assassination of the Emperor. In 1879 a woman and one
Leo Hartmann concocted a plot to blow up the imperial
train; they made a mistake and wrecked the wrong train,
which cost a number of innocent lives.

---

* *Nihil* is Latin; *Rien,* French; both mean the same, " *Nothing.*"

A second attempt was to dynamite the dining room at the Winter Palace. They did it at the wrong time and thirty lives of soldiers and servants were lost. The third attempt succeeded. Alexander II had progressed well with his great reforms and had attached his signature to a Constitution to be adopted by Russia. The next day a bomb was thrown at his carriage which killed and wounded a number of Cossacks, who accompanied the carriage. The Emperor in deep sympathy left the carriage to look at the dying men, when a second bomb blew him to pieces.

Among other assassinations traceable to nihilism and anarchism were the attempts to kill King Humbert of Italy, and Emperor William I of Germany. Later bomb outrages increased. President Carnot of France was stabbed at Lyons; the Empress of Austria and the King of Italy were murdered, also King Carlos and the Crown Prince of Portugal.

In Germany, Johann Most became the leader of the revolutionaries. He was expelled from Germany and went to London in 1879, where he shouted out the Marxian appeal: "Workers of the World Unite." He organized another secret society through which he aimed at a general revolution. He received no encouragement whatever in Great Britain at that time. It is far different today, thanks to the teachers of the Modernistic-Evolution theories. In 1880 the Society of the Illuminati was re-organized in Dresden, Saxony. It was done in such a secret manner that its existence only became known nineteen years later. Most and others were identified with it. In the same year a revolutionary congress was staged by Most in Switzerland. They worked in harmony with the Russian nihilistic assassination program, advocating world revolution in order to plunge the world into chaos.

The Social Democrats in Germany, coming more and more into power, differed but little from the Nihilistic-Anarchism; it was more subtle than the outspoken anarchy. Social Democracy shared with Anarchy the hatred of religion. The leading organ of Social Democracy the

"Socialdemokrat" on May 25, 1880 said: "It must be
candidly avowed Christianity is the bitterest enemy of
Social Democracy. When God is driven out of the brains
of men, the whole system of privilege by the grace of God
comes to the ground, and when heaven hereafter is recognized
as a big lie, men will attempt to establish heaven here.
Therefore, whoever assails Christianity assails, at the same
time, monarchy and capitalism." Most's headquarters
remained in England. But when he organized there a
revolutionary congress advocating a revolution after the
order of the Illuminati, proposing the annihilation of all
rulers and powers in authority, the clergy and all capitalists,
it was too much for patient England. After his arrest and
imprisonment for eighteen months he came to America.
There he attempted to develop his anarchy. The terrible
outrage in Chicago in 1886, the Haymarket tragedy, was
the fruitage of his agitations.

Fenianism appeared in Ireland with the same abolition
program, and England saw the inauguration of a number of
socialistic movements. A saving feature of Socialism was the
frequent quarrels amongst themselves, which divided them in
a number of factions. Then syndicalism came to the front as
well as the General Strike. According to Ramsay Macdonald,
the English Laborite, syndicalism is largely a revolt against
Socialism. But if we go deep enough we find beneath the
surface of syndicalism the developed creed of anarchy,
inasmuch as it rests upon the same basis—negation of the
State. The government by trades unions will lead to the
same goal as anarchy. The workers are to run not only
industries, but eventually the whole country. The great
method of syndicalism is the general strike. Here is the
plan as described in "World Revolution" and so often
disastrously carried out.

"First of all, a series of isolated strikes must take place in various
industries by way of partially paralyzing Capital and of unsettling
Labor. Then, at a given signal the workers, roused by violence, by
want and idleness, are to invade the workshops, mines, factories, etc.,
and take possession of them. At this stage of course the Government
will be obliged to call in the aid of police and soldiery and the fight will

begin. The revolutionaries will cut the telegraph and telephone lines; the railroads will be torn up to prevent transport of troops or provisions. By this means the Capital will be starved out, the markets will be empty, and the inhabitants rendered savage by hunger may be expected to turn on the Government and also on the bourgeoisie."*

In connection with the general strike, sabotage is advocated, the destruction of all kinds of machinery. To follow the history of the general strike, its successes, and more than that, its great failures, would take hundreds of pages.

Syndicalism is just another plan of world revolution. It is positively anti-patriotic, anti-democratic and anti-religious. In other words it is a propagation of the program out of the pit, the Satan-conceived Illuminism.

The second Internationale originated in 1889 in Paris. This was six years after Marx had died. May first was now constituted the day for revolutionary demonstration. Let us remember that Weishaupt organized his Illuminism on that day in 1776. It was altogether based upon his stolen theories, the revival of Weishaupt's and his followers' theories. Its leading feature was international Socialism. The World War arrested it temporarily, as most socialists still adhered to patriotism. As far as we have learned it is still in existence, but it was repudiated by the extreme, radical element, on account of being too friendly with the bourgeoisie. In 1903 a split took place. The left, or radical, wing of the Russian party obtained control and two groups were formed: The Bolsheviki, meaning "majority" and the Mensheviki, meaning "minority." From 1903 to 1918 there existed this Bolsheviki group, many of whom later became the leaders of the Soviet Red Republic. In the Zimmerwald Conference, held in 1915, a worshiper of Marx appeared, who became the awful leader of the Russian Revolution, in whom all the satanic efforts, the God and Christ opposition, since the eighteenth century were frightfully personified— *Nicolai Lenin.* On account of a younger brother, who was caught in a plot to kill the Czar and who

*"World Revolution," page 258.

was hanged for his crime, Lenin vowed eternal vengeance against all governments, society and civilization. Expelled from college on account of his revolutionary activities, exiled to Siberia, he lived obsessed by his great ambition of world revolution.

We have traced the workings of the mystery of lawlessness up to the Russian Revolution. The author believes, as stated before, that what is called "the end of the age" in Scripture had its first beginning in the revolutionary program of Weishaupt. Behind it are the powers of darkness, working towards the complete end of the age which is revealed in the Bible. Still God has kept back the full development of this mystery. We shall see in the chapters which follow how everything is now ready for the full, the most awful, manifestation of the powers of darkness.

CHAPTER VI

The Russian Revolution—Marxism Triumphant World-Revolution

The great world war broke out in August, 1914. It came at a time when our age had been lulled to sleep by the pacifist dreams of statesmen and deluded religious leaders, who preached an unscriptural and unreasonable optimism. The nations, generally called "Christian nations" all became involved. Even Bible-believing Christians missed one great lesson of the world war. It was a startling confirmation of the great prophecy the Son of God, our Lord Jesus Christ, had given in the shadow of the Cross. In announcing the character of the age, which follows His rejection by the Jews, He said: "Nation shall rise up against nation, and kingdom against kingdom; and there shall be famines, and pestilences and earthquakes, in divers places." This great prophecy had found a fulfilment in almost every century since it was spoken, but in the world war it was fulfilled as never before, the positive evidence that the age is, politically and morally, not getting better.

After the war had raged nearly three years a revolution came about in Russia. We term it the first revolution. We are not giving here the justifiable reasons of such a revolution which existed under the weakling Nicholas II, nor do we enter into the question what outside influences had a hand in it. It has been charged that Germany, in order to cripple Russia, had a great deal to do with the revolution. It is a fact that such was the case proved by damaging evidences. We leave this to a future historian who may be able to unravel the political intricacies of those days. Nor is it true that communism, springing from the godless Illuminati had anything to do with the dethronement of the Czaristic government. The Czar abdicated in March 1917 and as a result a provisional government was created. The people had elected a representative body, the "Duma," under the leadership of Prince Lvov. They took over the governmental affairs of Russia. Nicholas II abdicated to the Duma and neither Lenin, nor the Jew Trotzsky, had anything to do with it. Trotzsky lived under his right Jewish name—Bronstein—in New York and Lenin was an exile. The provisional government functioned under Kerensky from March to November 1917. The United States at once recognized the newly-founded Republic. Well does the author remember when the news reached our land that the Czar had stepped down, what jubilant expressions were given in the daily press, that Democracy, the rule by the people and for the people, had achieved another great triumph and that the world would soon be made "safe by democracy." What has become of all these nice little phrases? The writer, being in San Francisco, met a well-known citizen who expressed his great joy over the Russian revolution. We recollect our answer: "Russia is not ready for a well-ordered government by the people; I predict that probably another Czar will arise and if not, other coming revolutions will plunge Russia into an awful, an unspeakable, chaos." We spoke almost as a prophet, for the latter happened.

Russia had for years exiled the anarchistic-nihilistic-atheistic revolutionaries. The provisional government made the *terrible mistake* granting wholesale amnesty to this vicious element, and so they returned by the thousands. Their hour had come. That most terrible hour, which brought into history the greatest national tragedy! Among those who returned we find Lenin and Stalin and the Jew Trotzsky. The two former were exiles, one in Switzerland and the other in Siberia. Bronstein, alias Trotzsky, lived in the Bronx. In his last speech delivered in a hall, according to the press, he said: "I want you people to organize and keep on organizing in America in order that you may be able to overthrow this dirty, rotten government of the United States. I am going back to Russia to overthrow the government there, and stop this war with Germany." The Canadian government tried to arrest his return but he was released on the request of Kerensky. As to Lenin, with some thirty-five other revolutionaries, who had found shelter in

Switzerland, the German general staff acted, thinking that these revolutionists would undermine the morale of the army. They made possible their return to Russia, travelling from Switzerland through Germany in a sealed car. Then under the leadership of Lenin and Trotzsky, also Stalin, Zinovieff, another Hebrew, began planning their revolution. Just what the German general staff had anticipated happened. These leaders began to sow their seed among the disgruntled, war-weary troops, promising them almost everything including the division of all lands amongst them. In July 1917 a premature uprising ended in failure and Lenin and his associates had to flee to Finland. But soon they returned and staged an armed revolt in November of the same year. It was successful, for thousands of the army and navy had deserted and joined the revolution.

Kerensky, was far from being a leader; he was decidedly weak and was driven out, and the members of the government were either slaughtered or exiled. Then for several years the most horrible pages of all history were written. It was a continuation of the French revolution only on a gigantic scale. The reign of terror at the close of the eighteenth century was child's play in comparison with what happened in Russia. The teachings of the Satan-inspired Weishaupt and the equally vicious theories of the Jew, Karl Marx, were literally carried out. A war of extermination started and what had been suggested, as we stated in the preceding chapter, during the French revolution—the killing off of the population—became a horrible reality. Hundreds of thousands of the cultured, ruling classes and the bourgeoisie were murdered. Connected with it was a Satanic fury against religion, especially against Christianity, and a persecution of the Church began which is almost unsurpassed in the history of the Church. A police system was inaugurated, the *Cheka*, with the commission to torture, to kill without mercy. While the French reign of terror lasted a few months the Russian-Marxian atrocities continued for years.

The American Consul who resided in 1918 in Moscow sent on September the third a report to Washington describing the horrors. It was printed by our government in 1919 and is on file in Washington. We quote a paragraph:

"Since May the so-called Extra-ordinary Commission to combat counter-revolution has conducted an openly avowed campaign of terror. Thousands of persons have been summarily shot without even the form of trial. Many of them have, no doubt, been innocent of even the political views which were supposed to supply the motive of their execution."

The Consul stated at the close of the report: "The situation cries aloud to all who will act for the sake of humanity." But there was no action from the side of the so-called "Christian nations." The Jew Trotzsky was the main instigator of this program of hell, and he boldly justified the wholesale murdering "as a demonstration of the will and strength of the proletariat." This is a quotation from the official organ of the Bolsheviks, the *Isvestia* of January 10, 1919. And in the *Krasnaya Gazeta* (The Red Gazette) the president of the red army and the peasants' deputies wrote on August 31, 1918, an editorial urging the annihilation of the bourgeois class.

The man who wrote what we quote is a Jew by name of Apfelbaum, who, like the Weishaupt plotters, had changed his name to Zinovieff. He wrote these words: "The interests of the Revolution require the physical annihilation of the bourgeois class. It is time for us to start." A month later this violent, godless and apostate leader wrote in the same "Red Gazette":

"We will turn our hearts into steel, which we will temper in the fire of suffering and the blood of fighters for freedom. We will make our hearts cruel, hard, and unmovable, so that no mercy will enter them, and so that we will not quiver at the sight of a sea of enemy blood. We will let loose the floodgates of that sea. Without mercy, without sparing, we will kill our enemies in scores of hundreds."

These were not idle words. George Solomon, who was for a time as a diplomat, close to Lenin, Trotzsky, Krassin, Zinovieff and others, in his recently published volume describes this "hell on earth" he had to witness, mostly during the nights. The bloody work of the *Cheka*, was carried on in a certain large building. There the victims, men, women and children, were cruelly tortured before a shot ended their misery. In order to drown the despairing cries of the unfortunates, the building was surrounded with a number of powerful motor trucks; their motors were started and for hours they were kept agoing. Then night after night, week after week, for months, the almost countless hundreds of corpses were thrown into the trucks and carried away.

The very best people, the landowners, the members of the nobility, the middle class, and all who refused to fall in line with the program of the godless beasts, were killed off. We knew a number of the excellent Christians who perished at that time. Prince and Princesse Lieven were conse-crated Christians, Bible-loving believers, who did much good by their lives and testimonies. The whole family perished miserably. Some nine years ago a Christian gentleman, poorly clad, came to the office of the author. He introduced himself as a former Russian General, Vice-Admiral of the Russian Navy. He was grateful that he and his family escaped with their lives. We used him for several years in doing work among the Russians in New York City.

We have read the description of the horrors of these years in different languages. We shall not repeat them here nor describe the frightful, almost unbelievable suffer-ings of tens of thousands of boys and girls, who wandered aimlessly all over Russia, half starved, feeding on the carcasses of dead animals, perishing by the thousands. Nor shall we recite the rape of hundreds of girls and women, who were thrown into the arms of the revolutionary soldiery to satisfy their lust.*

It was difficult for the Church historian to give the correct number of the victims of the persecutions under the pagan

---

*Recently a volume has been published by an eye witness of many of these atrocities. We recommend it to our readers: "The Mystery of Iniquity," by Louis A. Pamount.

Roman Emperors, and it is difficult to give the number of
human beings who were murdered by the Bolsheviks. Con-
servative statisticians have given the number as one million
and eight hundred thousand. Others say that two million
and five hundred thousand comes nearer the truth.

Then Lenin, who had broken entirely with the second
socialist Internationale, formed the third Internationale
in Moscow to carry out the revolutionary program of the
Communist party and the Soviet Union. In January 1919
the revolutionary leaders of forty countries were called
to gather in Moscow.

The Internationale is known by the name of *Comintern*.
It has preserved the Illuminati program, advocating a social
world-wide revolution, instigating class warfare for the
purpose of creating a world sovietism with headquarters
in Moscow. Its aims are the very same as we have traced
in our previous chapter, the aims of Weishaupt, Babeuf,
and above all Karl Marx: Overthrow and annihilation of
all governments and capitalism; dictatorship of the proletariat; armed conflict of the proletariat against capitalism;
confiscation of property; complete separation from the
socialistic second Internationale. By-products are the
destruction of the family life through abolition of the marriage laws and easy divorce, advocating free love (known in
America as companionate marriage), the communal education of children. Another leading feature, which we shall
treat more fully, is hatred and complete destruction of the
Church, Christianity, the Bible, and all forms of Religion.
We retrace our steps. The first step is the theory of the
immoral Frenchman Rousseau, then comes Weishaupt with
his secret lodges of the Illuminati; then we step into the
French revolution, an expression of Illuminism; Karl Marx,
Lassale and Engels follow and the culminating expression
of this mystery of lawlessness, the realization of "the Communistic Manifesto" of Marx through the Russian
revolution.

This *Comintern*, the third Internationale, is like a terrible
Octopus which tries to encircle the whole world with its

slimy arms to pull down other nations into the whirlpool of destruction. To mention one of its many subsidiaries we call attention to the "Anti-Imperialistic World Congress" held under the auspices of Moscow in July 1929 in Frankfurt, Germany. The celebrated Professor Albert Einstein, whose figure disfigures a so-called "Christian Church" in New York City, was a member of this Moscow propaganda. His daughter, married to a Russian, is now in the land of the Soviets. "Einstein, the socialist, broadcasted his creed upon his arrival in the U. S. A., thereby proclaiming the real reason for his mission to our shores. The cloak of science slipped from his sloping shoulders, exposing underneath it the garment of Socialistic propaganda."*

We return to the story of the Russian revolution. Who staged the awful program? Who were the inhuman leaders who advocated mass-murder? The Bolsheviks are loud in praising Karl Marx. They are wedded to the "Communistic Manifesto." Most of the leaders of the Russian revolution of 1917-18 and the years following were Jews. This is no secret, in fact it is acknowledged by the Jews themselves. The *"Communist,"* a newspaper published in Kharkoff (April 12, 1919) makes the following boast:

"Without exaggeration, it may be said, that the great Russian Social Revolution was indeed accomplished by the hands of the Jews . . . It is true there are no Jews in the ranks of the Red Army as far as the privates are concerned, but in the committees and in the Soviet Organization, as Commissars, the Jews are gallantly leading the masses of the Russian proletariat to victory . . . The symbol of Jewry, which for centuries has struggled against capitalism, has become also the symbol of the Russian proletariat, which can be even seen in the face of the adoption of the Red five pointed star, which in former times, as it is well known, was the symbol of Zionism and Jewry."†

Nor is this the only boast. Another Communist organ, "The Red Gazette," says:

"The fundamental fact is incontestable, the Soviet bureaucracy is

*"T. N. T.," by Col. Edwin M. Hadley, page 67.
†More information can be had through Viscount Leon de Poncin's "The Secret Powers Behind the Revolution," London 1929.

almost entirely in the hands of Jews and Jewesses, whilst the number of Russians who participate in the government of the Soviets is ridiculously small."

A short time after the U. S. Consul in Moscow had given his report, our Government instituted an investigation through the Overman Committee in 1919. It is available to any citizen as a public document, the name of it is "Bolshevik Propaganda-Hearing Before the Sub-Committee of the Committee on the Judiciary, U. S. Senate, Sixty-Fifth Congress." Dr. George A. Simons, former superintendent of the Methodist Missions in Russia, was one of the chief witnesses before this Committee. Dr. Simons is personally known to the author, who can vouch for his reliability. He was in Russia as an American citizen during the Kerensky Government, and also during the Bolshevik revolution as a keen and intelligent observer. Dr. Simons gave some interesting information.[*]

"We were told that hundreds of agitators had followed in the trail of Trotzsky-Bronstein, these men having come over from the lower east side of New York. Some of them when they learned that I was the American pastor in Petrograd, stepped up to me and seemed very much pleased that there was somebody who could speak English, and their broken English showed that they had not qualified as being real Americans. A number of these men called on me and we were impressed with the strange Yiddish element in this thing right from the beginning, and it soon became evident that more than half of the agitators in the so-called Bolshevik movement were Jews. I do not want to say anything against the Jews as such. I am not in sympathy with the anti-Semitic movement, never have been, and do not ever expect to be. I am against it. But I have a firm conviction that this thing is Yiddish, and that one of its bases is found in the east side of New York."

It is a known fact that numbers of Jews went about that time from New York to Russia; they were said to be the followers of Bronstein, alias, Trotzsky. Dr. Simons continued:

"The latest startling information, given me by some one with good

_____
[*]We can quote only a small portion of the testimony given by him and by others.

authority, is this, that in December, 1918, in the northern community of Petrograd—that is what they call that section of the Soviet regime under the presidency of the man known as Apfelbaum (Zinovieff)—out of 388 members, only 16 happened to be real Russians, with the exception of one man, a negro from America who calls himself Professor Gordon.

"I was impressed with this, Senator, that shortly after the great revolution of the winter of 1917 there were scores of Jews standing on the benches and soap boxes, talking until their mouths frothed, and often remarked to my sister 'Well, what are we coming to, anyway? This all looks so Yiddish.' Up to that time we had very few Jews, because there was, as you may know, a restriction against having Jews in Petrograd; but after the revolution they swarmed in there and most of the agitators were Jews.

"I might mention this, that when the Bolsheviki came into power, all over Petrograd we at once had a predominance of Yiddish proclamations, big posters and everything in Yiddish. It became very evident that now that was to be one of the great languages of Russia; and the real Russians did not take kindly to it."

Dr. Simons then gave a partial list of the names of prominent leaders. We copy the list from the Report giving the Jewish name and the adopted Russian names in brackets.

Gutmann (Chernoff); Bronstein (Trotzsky); Zerbaum (Martoff); Katz (Kamkoff); Goldenberg (Meshkoff); Krochmal (Zagorsky); Gimmer (Suchanoff); (Dan Gurbitch); Geldfund (Parvuss); Sabelson (Kradek); Apfelbaum (Zinovieff); Nachkamkes (Stekloff); Lurye (Larin); Goldenbach (Ryanoff); Josse (Bogdanoff); Goldmann (Goryeff); Wanstein (Zwezdin); Goldmann (Lieber); Fuerstenberg (Ganezky); Solomon (Roshal). Litvinoff (Finkelstein).*

Other names could be added to this list of leaders of the Bolsheviki Revolution, all Jews. "One of the most curious features of the Bolshevist movement is the high percentage of non-Russian elements amongst its leaders. Of the twenty or thirty commissaries or leaders who provide the

*In the volume "The Cause of the World's Unrest" (London 1920), on pages 131 and 132 the leaders of the revolution in the very beginning are tabulated. Fifty men are mentioned their original names and nationalities and their pseudonyms are given. One is a woman. Of these 50 only six are Russians; one is a German and the other 43 are all Jews (the woman a Jewess). The list, this book states, "is the result of much labor and the work of several persons."

central machinery of the Bolshevist movement not less than 75% are Jews" (*London Times*, March 29, 1919). And there are many other witnesses to the same effect too numerous to quote. A widely known French Journal "*L'Ilustration*" had on September 14, 1918 an article in which the following facts are given:

"When one lives in contact with the functionaries who are serving the Bolshevist Government, one feature strikes the attention, which is, that almost all of them are Jews. I am not at all anti-semitic, but I must state what strikes the eye: everywhere in Petrograd, in Moscow, in provincial districts, in all commisariats, in district offices, in Somlny, in the former ministries, in the Soviets, I have met nothing but Jews and again Jews . . . The more one studies the second revolution the more one is convinced that Bolshevism is a Jewish movement which can be explained by the special conditions in which the Jewish people were placed in Russia."

In the "British White Book on Bolshevism in Russia," published in 1919 the same information is found by the most reliable witnesses. "Witnesses further stated that the Bolshevik leaders did not represent the Russian working classes, most of them being Jews." Nor must we overlook the fact that when in 1919 a Communist Government was established in Hungary, the directorate of five included four Jews. The Secretary was a Jew and Szamuelly, the head of the terrorist troops was a Jew. The leader Bela Kuhn (Cohn) was a friend of Trotzsky. The "*Jewish Chronicles*" of April 4, 1919 made the admission of all this— "There is much in the fact of Bolshevism itself that so many Jews are Bolshevists, in the fact that the ideals of Bolshevism at many points are consonant with the *finest ideals of Judaism.*"

The two outstanding leaders were Lenin and Bronstein-Trotzsky. Lenin's claim of belonging to the Russian nobility has been disproved, but it is said that he was born of a Jewish mother. Lenin was the greatest worshipper of Karl Marx. His "Communistic Manifesto" became the guide of Lenin, he followed it closely and Marxism was enthroned in the Bolshevik Revolution. Nor is Jewish leadership abandoned in 1933, for the press but recently announced that a Mr.

Kaganowitch, a Jew, who hates God and Christianity, has been chosen as the successor to the present dictator Stalin.

And now we have to say something about that extremely mysterious document known as *"The Protocols of the Elders (or Wise Men) of Zion."* This document first came to light about 16 years before the first Russian Revolution. It was published by a Russian, Serge Nilus in 1901 and passed through a number of editions. A copy was deposited in the British Museum in 1907. The information as to Nilus is meagre. We have seen the title page of one of these original editions and that page gives a strong indication that the man was a believer in the Word of God, in prophecy, and must have been a true Christian.

The title is *"It is Near at the Door."* Then we noticed the following Scripture passages printed on the title page: Matthew xxiv:33; Mark xiii:29; Luke xxi:31; Revelation i:3; xxii:10; Daniel xii:4. On the rest of this page we find the following statements: *"Concerning something people do not wish to believe and which is so near."* Fourth edition of the book "Near is the Coming of Antichrist and the Kingdom of the Devil on Earth." Revised and considerably augmented by later Researches and investigation. *"Dedicated to the Small Herd of Christ."* Finally two other passages are quoted in full: 1 Thessalonians v:4 and Matthew xxiv:13.

Furthermore in reading these "Protocols" as contained in the book of Nilus, one becomes deeply convinced that an humble man of the stamp of Nilus could not possibly have written such a deeply worded document. The reading of these Protocols impresses one rather that they are the work of a set of very able men, students of history, of economics, finances and world politics. But the most important fact is that throughout the twenty-four Protocols we have a *very pronounced re-statement of the principal theories of Illuminism and Marxism.*

They have been branded a forgery by Jews and Gentiles. The authorship of this serious document will, in the opinion of the writer, never be ascertained. The words of the father of

modern Zionism, Dr. Theodor Herzl, advocating the Jewish
state, saying—"When we sink we become a revolutionary proletariat," are insufficient to link Zionism with the Protocols,
as it has been attempted.   But the advocated plan of World
Domination and World Revolution is a most sinister one.
And here is the most astonishing fact, nearly all that these
Protocols advocate, the destruction of Christian civilization,
has at least partially been brought about by the Revolution
and Sovietism.   The work of undermining is still followed.
A painstaking and deeper study of the Protocols, compared
with present day world conditions, must lead, and does
lead, to the conviction, that the plan of the Protocols, whoever concocted it, is not a *crude forgery*.   Behind it are
hidden, unseen actors, powerful and cunning, who follow
the plan still, bent on the overthrow of our civilization.*

We cannot enter into a detail examination of this question,
though the author, after years of study of this question is
well fitted to do this.   But we shall now quote a few of the
high-points found in the Protocols.   Reader!   Do not pass
over these pages lightly.   Compare these statements with
what is going on in the world of today.

In our day the *power of gold* has replaced liberal rulers.   There was
a time when faith ruled.   The idea of freedom cannot be realized
because no one knows how to make reasonable use of it.   Give the
people self-government for a short time and it will become corrupted.
From that very moment strife begins and soon develops into social
struggles, as a result of which states are aflame and their authority is
reduced to ashes.

The people of the Gentiles are stupefied by spirituous liquors; their
youth is driven insane through excessive studies of the classics, and
vice to which they have been instigated by our agents-tutors, valets,
governesses—in rich houses, by clerks and so forth, and by our women
in the pleasure places of the Gentiles.   Among the latter I include the
so-called "society women," their volunteer followers in vice and luxury.
Our motto is power and hypocrisy.   Only power can conquer in

---

*About ten years ago a leading New York publisher was to publish
an edition of the Protocols.   When the book was about to be issued
several prominent Jews threatened to ruin the publisher's business if
he dared to circulate the Protocols.   He was intimidated and recalled
the publication.

politics . . . Violence must be the principle; hypocrisy and cunning the rule of those governments which do not wish to lay down their crowns at the feet of the agents of some new power. The evil is the sole means of attaining the goal of good.* For this reason we must not hesitate at bribery, fraud and treason when these can help us to reach our end. In politics it is necessary to seize the property of others without hesitation if in so doing we attain submission and power.

By the severity of our doctrines, we shall triumph and shall enslave all governments under our super-government. Even in olden times we shouted among the people "Liberty, Equality, Fraternity." These words have been repeated so many times since by unconscious parrots, which, flocking from all sides to the bait, have ruined the prosperity of the world and true individual freedom, formerly so well protected from the pressure of the mob.

In all parts of the world the words "Liberty, Equality, Fraternity" have brought whole legions into our ranks through our blind agents, carrying our banners with delight. Meanwhile these words were worms which ruined the prosperity of the Gentiles, everywhere destroying peace, quiet, and solidarity, undermining all foundations of their states . . . Abstract liberty offered the opportunity for convincing the masses that government is nothing but the manager representing the owner of the country, namely the people, and that this manager can be discarded like a pair of worn out gloves.

Do not think that our assertions are without foundation: note the successes of Darwinism, Marxism and Nietzscheism *engineered by us. The demoralizing effects of these doctrines* upon the minds of the Gentiles should already be obvious to us.

We have opened the arenas in different states, where revolts are now occurring, and *disorders and bankruptcy will shortly appear everywhere.*

We will present ourselves in the guise of saviours of the workers from oppression when we suggest that they enter our army of Socialists, Anarchists, Communists, to whom we always extend our hand under the guise of the rule of the brotherhood demanded by the human solidarity of our social masonry.

This hatred will be still more accentuated by the *economic crisis which will stop financial transactions and all industrial life.*

Having organized a general economic crisis by all possible underhand means and with the help of gold which is all in our hands, we will throw great crowds of workmen on the street, simultaneously, in all countries of Europe. These crowds will gladly shed the blood of those of whom they, in the simplicity of their ignorance, have been jealous since childhood and whose property they will then be able to loot. They

---

*One of Weishaupt's principles was "The end justifies the means." It is echoed in Marxism.

will not harm our people (Jews) because we will know of the time of attack and we will take measures to protect them.

Remember the French Revolution, which we have called "great," the secrets of its preparation are well known to us, for it was the work of our hands. Since then we have carried the masses from one disappointment to another, so that they will renounce even us in favor of a despot sovereign of Zionist blood, whom we are preparing for the world.

To control public opinion it is necessary to perplex it by the expressions of numerous contradictory opinions until the Gentiles get lost in the labyrinth, and come to understand that it is best to have no opinions of political questions.

The aristocracy of the Gentiles as a political force is dead. We do not need to take it into consideration. But as landowners they are harmful to us because they can be independent in their resources of life. *For this reason we must deprive them of their land at any cost.*

Let us raise wages, which, however, will be of no benefit to the workers, for we will simultaneously cause the rise in prices of objects of first necessity under the pretext that this is due to the decadence of agriculture, and of the cattle industry.

We have misled, corrupted, fooled, and demoralized the youth of the Gentiles by education along principles and theories known by us to be false but which we ourselves have inspired.

In countries so-called advanced we have created insane, dirty and disgusting literature.

Today freedom of religion has been proclaimed everywhere, consequently, *it is only a question of a few years before the complete collapse of Christendom.*

We must extract the very conception of God out of the minds of the Christians . . . We must destroy all professions of faith . . . We have taken great care to discredit the clergy of the Gentiles in the eyes of the people, and thus have succeeded in injuring their mission, which could have been very much in our way. The influence of the clergy is diminishing daily. Today freedom of religion prevails everywhere, but the time is only a few years off when Christianity will fall to pieces.

We will destroy the family life of the Gentiles . . . We will also distract them by various kinds of amusements, games, pastimes, passions, public houses.

You know that the gold currency was detrimental to the governments that accepted it, for it could not satisfy the requirements for money *since we took as much gold as possible out of circulation.*

These are a very few and imperfect quotations from this sinister document; we could add scores more. The whole scheme has been put into practice. The world is in its grasp. The forces behind it are the forces of unrighteousness and lawlessness. God knows the unseen and unknown enemies. He who has set the bounds for the sea-waves has the power and means to restrain these evil men, the serpent's seed, and as we show later in our work, the time of the complete defeat of the old serpent and its seed will surely come.

One of the favored utterances of Karl Marx is concerning religion. *"Religion is the opium of the people."* He was anti-religion, anti-church, anti-Christ and anti-Bible. Lenin, Trotzsky-Bronstein and the others, furiously followed the anti-religious and anti-Christian ravings of Marx and the whole Socialistic-Anarchistic-Communistic movements. In the beginning there seemed to be some toleration, but the most vicious element of the Soviets gained the upper hand and now the five year plan of the *godless*, counting already millions of members, has set the year 1937 when not a single church, or house of prayer is to be left in the Soviet dominions. There have been blasphemies in the past, unspeakable blasphemies, but the godless Soviets have manifested a Satanic Christ-hating, Christ-despising spirit, which is even unknown in the French revolution. Some of the colored cartoons published, in the possession of the author, are extremely vile. One of them pictures our Lord in a wheelbarrow with a bottle of wine and a loaf of bread, about to be dumped upon a refuse-heap by a Red. Others are even worse.

At first the persecution seemed to be aimed at the destruction of the orthodox Greek Church, for the orthodox Church under the Czarist government had been instrumental in the persecution of the Jews and others, hence the revolutionaries turned first of all against that Church and planned its complete destruction. Among the 1,766,118 victims up to the beginning of 1922, figures obtained from the Soviet documents, nearly five thousand were priests, teachers, nuns, etc., of the Greek Church. The Metropolitan of Kieff, Archbishop Anthony (*London Times*, April 18, 1920) wired to the Archbishop of Canterbury: "From 1917 to 1920 the Bolshevists killed one Metropolitan, five Archbishops, sixteen Bishops, thirteen shot, nine tortured cruelly to death." But soon the persecution extended to the millions of Lutheran, Reformed, Baptist, Methodist and especially the Mennonite Christians. The president of the Lutheran world conference, Dr. John A. Morehead, addressing an audience in 1932 in New York City, told of the martyrdom of Lutherans under the regime of the Reds. There are a million Lutherans in Russia and only eighty-one pastors are remaining. Of these forty are still at liberty and forty-one are in prisons and exiled. In a little cemetery in Riga, Latvia, is a marble slab with the names of forty-two Lutheran pastors, murdered in 1918 when the Red beasts invaded the Baltic provinces. Nearly 100,000 Lutherans live banished, in semi-starvation in Siberia. The World Conference sent them a pastor. While he was leaving a home, where he had ministered to a sick family, he was murdered. Then in England and America great protest meetings were held denouncing this horrible program of the godless demons. The American Soviets with their "baptized infidel" backing, the miserable, un-American "Pinks" who call themselves "The Friends of the Soviets" started an opposition meeting, which meant an endorsement of the Red Anti-Christian propaganda. One of the speakers announced was the former Episcopal Bishop of Arkansas, William Montgomery Brown, now Communist. About that time the following was broadcast from Moscow:

"The All-Union Society of Militant Atheists has drawn up an ambitious five-year anti-religious program, envisaging a total membership of 35,000,000 by 1933. It now has nearly 3,000,000 members, and it estimates that part of the new membership will be 18,000,000 children between the ages of eight and fourteen.

"The society plans a chain of anti-religious educational institutions and the appointment of anti-religious faculties in the state universities at Moscow, Leningrad and elsewhere. Organized bodies of atheistic agitators and propagandists will be trained there.

"Special anti-religious films, radio programs, theatrical performances exhibitions in museums and a large number of itinerant anti-religious units will be prepared.

"Planetariums, showing materialistic construction of the world as opposed to spiritual, will be constructed at Leningrad, Kharkov, Sverdlovsk, Novosibirsk, Frunze and Tiflis, similar to the one now in Moscow.

"Three full operas, four operettas, eleven reviews, thirteen musical comedies, twenty vaudeville sketches and twelve children's plays lampooning religion and deriding the Church will be produced in the next two years. Special anti-religious theatrical companies will travel throughout the union holding religion up to ridicule.

"Thirty anti-religious paintings and sculptures by widely known artists will be made. Atheistic newspapers and magazines will be published in seventeen languages. State factories, collective farms and other Soviet institutions, consisting entirely of atheistic workmen, will be created. Fifteen crematories will be built in Moscow and other large cities. Practical measures will be taken to introduce a new calendar to replace the present religious calendar."

Well did Bishop Manning say: "I believe we are facing today one of the greatest crises in Christian history. The Russian warfare against God is not confined to that land; its influence is being felt throughout the world." How true! The old serpent, Satan, the devil and dragon is rising up for the final battle, which precedes his complete defeat.

Perhaps the greatest sufferers as Christians have been the Mennonites. For many years they had in southern Russia prosperous settlements; they were law abiding and earnest believers. The author was in touch with them years ago through his German publications and knew a good many of them. What horrible sufferings, torture and death, this good people have passed through! Whole villages were wiped out. And today hundreds of them are confined in miserable prison camps, suffering untold agonies. And in the wilds of Siberia, in the far north, hundreds of thousands of other banished ones are still living enslaved, deprived of all the needed simple comforts of life, degraded and half starved. The suffering of the thousands of women is simply indescribable. Thousands of churches of the different branches have been demolished and the work of destruction goes on, so that as stated before, by 1937 not a single church building or meeting house is to be left. Those who oppose and continue to preach the Gospel are dealt with in the most cruel manner. Thousands are deported, and among the 500,000 confined in the far northern Solovetsky Island are hundreds of evangelical ministers.

Hundreds of thousands are even in a worse condition in Russia itself. In order to make purchases of the necessities of life, bread, milk, meat and other victuals, cards are issued. These are withheld from hundreds of thousands, who are not in sympathy with the godless program, or who adhere to any form of religion, and they are thus systematically starved. Even the Soviet workers themselves are suffering for want of sufficient food, for the godless Utopia, has turned out, as some returning American engineers have testified "hell on earth." Mrs. Clarence Warren, who spent with her husband, a California engineer, some time in the land of Sovietism, according to our New York dailies, gave the following testimony:

"Fear is on all sides. Millions would not be surprised if they were flung suddenly into the state of starvation which would drive them into a state of cannibalism. They have abolished God there, and you would have to be there to know what that means. They have tried to destroy spiritual hope as they have destroyed earthly hope. There is no religion there and churches are mocked at. Marriage is a civil ceremony and not often that. It is the most immoral country I have ever been in. Even Americans are contaminated. The peasants are treated like dogs and the peasant women like animals lower than dogs."

And the unfortunates who, in order to satisfy the pitiful cries of their children for bread, tried to get it in an illegal way, were treated as enemies, and as endorsing a counter-revolution. Cases upon cases are reported when the obtaining of a loaf of bread in an improper way was punished by death. Only recently fifteen were executed, including two women, because they had gone to a freight car in search for some food and clothing to hide their nakedness.

Needless to say, the printing of religious periodicals, the advertisment of religious books, the circulation of the Bible, and any form of religious activity, is not only strictly forbidden, but punishable with exile.

One of the most Satanic schemes is the corruption of the

young. All religious instruction, including the reading of the Bible in a home to young children under the age of eighteen, is punishable with compulsory labor for a period of one year. As a result all religious schools have been closed. Our Mennonite brethren, also the Baptists and other evangelicals have continued heroically to preach Christ.

Several years ago the author received from Russian believers, information which was subsequently published in "*Our Hope*."

"Tutchkoff, one of the foremost Christ-haters, said: 'The most formidable enemies of the Soviet power are the Evangelical Christians Baptists and others. They preach of a Christ that has never been, as well as a God, and thereby lead their people into slavery. Not much time remains, we shall annihilate you, branches, root and all; if there exists a devil, we are with him!'

"I remember another case. It was a very blessed meeting we held from which some communists had fled. The next day they came to me and said '*We shall not rest until we are immersed to the breast in your Christian blood*'."*

But while the Soviets antagonize all instruction of Children in religious matters, they attend themselves to sowing the seeds of atheism in the hearts of the young. They invented an elaborate system of an anti-Christian education for the coming generation. A catechism begins with the question, "Is there a God? Answer: No." Then follow questions and answers which attempt to show that capitalism and the Church are one and that they are the enemies of humanity. We quote from the "*Koelnische Zeitung*" some reliable, first hand information:†

"The first stage in the formation of the Russian child mind is that of the kindergarten. The kindergarten plays so important a part in Russia, because the Russian child must go to school only after it has reached the eighth or ninth year.

"Family life, owing to the participation of women in outside vocations, and owing further to the lack of living-quarters, is quite disintegrated.

---

*From "Our Hope," May, 1930.

†From "Our Hope," April, 1932.

"In almost every street one will see a 'kindergarten' sign. There the children play in really nice rooms and learn to read and write. And in the kindergarten the formation of the child mind along Bolshevik lines is made to begin with the assurance in the simplest letters of the alphabet that there is no God.

"Many children bring to the Bolshevik kindergartens and primary schools certain religious preconceptions imbibed in the homes of their parents. Effective combating of such parental ideas has led to the introduction of a kind of instruction which is in fact anti-religious propaganda. Through the children it is planned to influence parents and guardians.

"By this means, as the Bolsheviks believe, they can make some headway against the deeply religious tendencies which still persist among the masses of the Russian people.

"The reading lessons of the children take on thus a strongly marked hostility to religious ideas. These lessons are directed against 'priestly morals and their class nature,' against 'religion and the maladies it fosters,' against 'the slave,' meaning by this the connection between religion and the servitude of the peasants in the old bad days, the whole concluding with a course in 'words and acts of the pastors.'

"Pains are taken to impress upon the children the view that religion was but a device to keep the people in a state of ignorant stupidity, and that the Church was an institution which took the last coin out of the pockets of the poor."

One of the tricks played on the children is to let them get very hungry. They are then told to pray to God and he will send them bread. So the innocents begin to pray little prayers to God for bread. But nothing happens. In the room is a picture of the Soviet god, the idol, Lenin. The children are told he will give them something to eat. Then suddenly, after they have looked to that lost soul, the bread appears.

But is this Satanic work confined to Russia? Socialistic-Communistic schools (called in mockery "Sunday-Schools") are arising throughout our own land. They have *lessons*; here are samples: Capitalist Murders—Red Flag—French revolution. They have *hymns*: "Arise ye starvelings"—"The Internationale"—"The Marseillaise". They have a *doxology*: "No Saviors from on high deliver." They have *saints*: Lenin and the other followers of Marx. God is blasphemed, the Bible ridiculed and Christ dishonored. The Soviets have several youths' organizations. These are reproduced in the United States in the "Young Communist League" and the "Young Pioneers." They hate and despise our all American Boy Scouts and Girl Scouts. How they function may be learned from the following incident of four years ago.

Fifty children led by a few adults brought out the police reserves yesterday when their communistic banners and speeches of belligerence chided 239 Boy Scouts setting sail on the Cunarder *Samaria* for the International Boy Scout jamboree at Birkenhead, England.

The reserves were necessary because the children, many of them girls from ten to fifteen years of age, turned a scuffle into a riot when they tore into a crowd of men who attempted to prevent the leaders of the communists from making speeches.

There were 2,000 men and women on the pier to see friends sail on the *Samaria*. Many of these were drawn into the free-for-all when traffic policemen, called from the street, forced the battling children down the pier.

Girls hardly four feet tall used fists and fingernails as the police tore from their hands banners that advised the Boy Scouts to desert that organization for the Young Pioneers, communistic society to which the paraders belong.

This was repeated on March 6, 1930, in Union Square. Children, carrying inflammatory banners, attacked the police. Girls scratched and bit policemen, spat at them and used vile language. A riot followed in which the police on the advice of Police Commissioner Grover A. Whalen acted, as one officer was almost murdered. The red, God and man defying leaders, were jailed. What happened next? Certain men and women who call themselves American citizens objected to the Commissioner's "high-handed, unwarranted and illegal methods in dealing with the communists when force was used quelling the riot." Among the sympathizers appears prominently Dr. Henry Sloane Coffin, the President of that hotbed of American modernism, Union Theological Seminary, New York City.*

And Moscow continues its program of undermining the political, the social and religious life of different nations.

*"Our Hope," May, 1930.

To accomplish the "world revolution," the domination of the world by the demonized teachings of Karl Marx, this country must fall, they say, as Russia fell.

Joseph Stalin has published last year a detailed plan for the destruction of our country. This information was passed on to all the Communistic District organizers and secretaries throughout our country. Read it! Then review in your mind what has taken place and what is increasingly taking place all over our country and note the actions of certain Congressmen and Senators. Then decide for yourself the seriousness of the situation. Here are the devil's suggestions:

Religion: By philosophy, mysticism, the development of liberal cults, and the furtherance of atheism, to discredit all Christian creeds.

Ethical: Corrupt morality by advocating promiscuity and advising high school and university students to practice same; introduction of companionate marriage ideas; advocation of legalized abortions; advancement of theoretical interracial practices—marriage of white women to colored men—by actual consummation through willing participants where obtainable. Destruction of the family, abolition of inheritance, even to the extent of names; destruction of all records of title, birth and family history.

Aesthetic: Cultivation of the ugly, futuristic and aberrant in art, literature, the drama and music; the practice of crude orientalism, modernism and degenerate perversion.

Sociological: Abolition of social opposition by subversive practices; the display of vulgar extravagance, promotion and exaggeration of all social and economic conditions, political corruption, etc., to create unrest, suspicion and revolt by the workers, intensify class war.

Industrial and Financial: Create mistrust of banks by circulation of rumors of instability and distress. Destroy ideals in craftsmanship and pride of workmanship; set up—by series of public talks by professors of sociology and others—the picture of a golden serpent of profit. Standardization of the cheap and shoddy; advocate the state monopoly of ownership; exchange of all foreign currency at slight discount for U. S. gold and gradually withdraw gold from circulation, send all gold currency to Russia.

Political: Set up the ideal of thinking "internationally," so as to undermine national patriotism; weaken all government departments by corruption. Attack all political parties and create suspicion and distrust upon any and all occasions. Amplify facts by fiction and create startling exposures. Ridicule all patriotic effort and undermine all preparation for defense; carry out our set policy for world revolution outlined in Rykoff's position.

Rykoff, in "Pravda," said: "It is our duty to inculcate in the minds of all nations the theory of international friendship, pacifism and disarmament, at the same time, however, never for one moment relaxing our efforts in the upbuilding of our own military establishment."

Lenin said: "When a country is selected for attack we must first set up before the youth of that land a mental barrage which will forever prohibit the possibility of that youth being moulded into an armed force to oppose our invading armies. This can most successfully be done through creating 'war horror' thought and by teaching of pacifism and non-resistance. It will be found that powerful organizations of non-communists can be created for this purpose particularly with the aid of liberal-minded ministers, professors and lecturers."

Bucharin said: "Friendship of liberal-minded ministers shall be sought, as these men are at the present time the leaders of the masses.

Conferences on economic conditions among the people shall be held from time to time with these ministers, educators and other liberal elements and through their influences the party shall aim to secure a more favorable hearing before the people."

Read it once more! All that is advocated by these enemies of God and man is being carried out today in the United States and elsewhere. Look deeper and see how the industrial and financial experiences of the world during the last three years are *linked up with this program.* It is not a new program. It is the program of the Illuminati, the program of the French revolution, of Babeuf and Karl Marx. And the liberal-minded ministers, educators and others, who call themselves "The Friends of the Soviet," have responded to this program. Hundreds of preachers of the modernistic-materialistic-evolution type, who are infidels, men who have abandoned the true Gospel of Jesus Christ and turned socialists, with hundreds more of college professors and high school teachers, are now playing into the hands of the reds, advocating the introduction of the devil-inspired theories of Marx-Lenin-Trotzsky and Stalin. How can any self-respecting man or woman, not to speak of Christians, advocate the recognition of the Soviets by our government, so that the flag of honor and glory, can be displayed alongside the red flag of blood, murder and ruin?

The great effort of the Soviets is to cripple our nation through Pacificism. For several years the emissaries of the reds, like Litvinoff, have advocated a clean-cut disarmament program. They are at it again. Our modernistic educators, and unpatriotic modernistic preachers, fall in line with it and as a result, as we shall show in our next chapter, our youth is falling more and more into the Pacifist trap. But what is the naked truth? The Soviets desire disarmament, crippling the defense forces of what they call "Capitalistic Governments" so that when the right moment comes for the planned uprising and a repetition of the Russian revolution is brought about, no state militia or U. S. Army can defend the helpless bourgeoisie.

We state nothing but facts. Here is the program of Moscow. The Soviets have three million men under arms; five and a half million belong to the reserves and are available at any time. They boast that by October first of this year (1933) they expect to have seventeen million citizens engaged in some form of military and aviation activity under a new five-year plan for aerial and chemical defense. No other nation has the well-equipped aeroplanes of every description that Russia has. Several million women also receive systematic instruction in elementary military service, gas warfare and red cross nursing. This is the brand of pacifism the reds have produced. It is true the leaders of the reds, the slave-holders of the millions, whom they have forced to bow to their will, are deadly afraid of an internal revolution, which would end their domination. But on the other hand this great military outfit is held in reserve for the anticipated world-revolution. All honor to the "*Chicago Tribune,*" which had recently the following editorial:

"The soviet government through its commissar of foreign affairs proposes the abolition of the 'most aggressive types of armament,' including tanks, heavy artillery, ships of more than 10,000 tons, naval artillery of more than 12-inch caliber, aircraft carriers, military dirigibles, heavy bombing planes, etc.—in short, all implements of modern warfare which Soviet Russia is short of and least able to acquire.

"All that the soviet would have on these terms would be the largest reserve of man power of any nation in Europe, controlled by a fanatic nucleum of disciplined bolshevik troops.   The soviet is for complete disarmament.   It can well afford to favor it for the same reason.   If there were no modern weapons at all requiring technical skill to make, the power of a Russian horde would be proportionately that much greater.   Civilized European nations would be at its mercy.

"Communists like to talk about capitalist or bourgeois hypocrisy. There is no hypocrisy in history more flagrant than the bolshevik dictatorship's pretense of devotion to peace.   The bolshevik regime was established by force and waded through blood to power.   It is maintained today by arms and dares not meet the criticism and publicity of free speech or a free press.   It has destroyed liberty of thought and conscience and the peace it has created is the peace of any other tyranny, the peace of the sword.   As for world peace, it is carrying on throughout the world an organized conspiracy against the peace of every other nation, and the conspiracy is to foment violence, to plan and precipitate riots, to inflame hatred, create secret treachery, to break down the agencies of public order, and thus to give opportunity for ruthless minorities ready to seize power by slaughter and hold it by arms.

"Bolshevism is the enemy of peace in every other nation.   After nearly fifteen years of mastery in Russia, and in spite of its vaunted betterments, it dares not meet the challenge of free thought and speech. Its rule is the rule of armed might.   When its emissary appears at Geneva, bolshevism holds up the dove of peace with bloody hands."

We wonder if Bishop Francis McConnell of the Methodist Church, Sherwood Eddy, John Haynes Holmes, Harry Emerson Fosdick and several thousand other preachers and college professors have read it.   They should, and take it to heart.

Before the writer is a mass of material of other nature shedding light upon what is going on in Russia and elsewhere through the red propaganda.   It is an impossibility to mention it all.   Our next chapter will uncover the menace we are facing.

In concluding this chapter we mention the fact that the emblems of the reds are a *hammer* and a *sickle*.   Well chosen!   They are instruments of death and destruction. But there is another hammer and another sickle.   That other hammer will strike some day; there is another sickle which will become active in mighty power.   Then all ye godless, ye leaders of the world revolution, your hour has come. "Is not My Word like a *hammer* that breaks the rock to pieces?" (Jer. xxiii:29). His Word will be manifested ere long as the Judge in the manifestation of Him, Who is the Word of God. Of Him it is written: "And I looked, and behold, a white cloud, and upon the cloud one sat like unto the Son of Man, having on His Head a golden Crown and in His Hand a sharp *sickle*. And another angel came out of the Temple, crying with a loud voice to Him that sat on the cloud, Thrust in Thy sickle and reap, for the time is come for thee to reap. And He that sat on the cloud thrust in His sickle on the earth and the earth was reaped" (Rev. xiv:14-16). The harvest in the end of the age is fast approaching.

CHAPTER VII

The Revolutionary Propaganda in the United States

The program of Sovietism is the program of world-revolution. This is not a secret. The trumpets of Moscow have blared it for years. The red agitators are found in every continent. They are active among the Mongolian races in the far East. They sow their seed of hate in India. In Central Asia they have been partially successful. Africa is feeling it and the black races are stirred by it. Throughout Europe the agents of Sovietism are found in every country. If it had not been for the recent events in Germany that country would probably have been plunged into a red revolution, which would have cost many thousands of lives. It was Mussolini who saved Italy from a similar fate. In France, England, Spain, Austria, Bulgaria, Roumania and all other European countries the red agitators are active. In Australia, South America, Central America, in Mexico and Canada have the same experience and fight the encroaching Communism.

According to the claims of Russia successful revolutionary propaganda is now carried on in fifty countries. But the country which is in the grasp of communistic intrigues as perhaps no other civilized country, is the United States. Communism has become a *menace*, greater than any other menace in the past and present history of our republic.

It used to be said, and people believed it, that when the ostrich is pursued by hunters and the pursuit becomes hotter, that the bird, in order to escape the consciousness of danger, buries its head in the sand. It is a zoological myth. No animal is so stupid as that. But our government for a number of years has played the alleged ostrich feat, and talked itself into the dream that there is no danger, refusing to believe that the agitation of the lawless ones could affect our "glorious country." Ever since the congressional investigation under the able leadership of the Hon. Hamilton Fish, Jr., has uncovered the nation-wide activities of the enemy within our gates there has been an awakening. Yet some of our legislators slumber on, while others are opposing the legislations needed to crush out the open and secret activities of the seed of the serpent, advocating the overthrow of our government, and the establishment of a Soviet government under the direct domination of Moscow. The fullest awakening to this horrible menace has not yet come. May it not be far away when our country will be purged from the agitators from abroad and still more so from a certain class of American citizens, who have aligned themselves with the Soviets to assist them in their vicious propaganda.

Communism is now a political party in the United States. It was founded in Chicago in September 1919 by a number of the extreme American radicals and is a part of the third Internationale. It was composed almost entirely of foreign born workers. A short time later it was forced into hiding on account of its illegality. Then in December 1921 the Communist party was camouflaged under the name "Workers Party of America," but in 1928 the mask was thrown aside and they came out into the open as the "Communist Party of America" in full allegiance with Moscow and the Comintern. And here we must quote from the congressional report:*

The communists came more and more into the open until today they flaunt their revolutionary activities throughout the country. Since 1925 the Department of Justice has had no power, no authority, or funds from the Congress to investigate communist propaganda or activities. During the period that the Department of Justice had actual authority the Communist Party was driven underground where it could not function successfully. Just so long as the agents of the Department of Justice were active the movement remained comparatively stationary and innocuous. At the present time the Communist Party of the United States is thoroughly and highly organized, nationally and locally, and is extremely active.

This shows how thoroughly asleep our government has been and how it has permitted a revolutionary party, under

_____
*Congressional Report No. 2290, page 9.

outside, non-American domination and control, to carry on its program of destruction of our government, our industries, the American family, our patriotism, our Churches and our schools. The trail of the serpent has become most prominent in our country. The astonishing growth of communism, this offspring of Marx, Weishaupt and other godless elements, we shall now briefly follow. Who does not desire in view of it to cry out with a loyal American citizen and writer—"In God's Name why do we Americans permit the working of red Russia's conspiracies in this country? Have we lost the sturdy stamina of our forefathers?"*

W. Z. Foster, several times candidate for the presidency on the communistic ticket, has voiced in clear language what the object of this party is. In his acceptance speech in 1928 he said:

"The working class must shatter the capitalistic state. It must build a new state, a new government, a workers' and farmers' government, the Soviet Government of the United States. No communist, no matter how many votes he should secure in the national election, could, even if he would, become president of the present government. When a communist heads a government in the United States, and that day will come just as surely as the sun rises, that government will not be a capitalistic government, but a Soviet government, and behind this government will stand *the red army to enforce the dictatorship of the proletariat.*"

This same radical, in the investigation of the congressional committee revealed the fact how completely the communistic party is under the control of Moscow. He also made it clear that they only own one flag, not the flag of the United States, but the red flag.

How highly organized this alien party has become may be learned from the fact that the "Trade Unity League," a section of the Red Internationale, has in the United States over seventy-five organizations affiliated with communism.

All the leading industries are represented—agriculture, clothing workers, metal and iron workers, cleaning and

---

*"T. N. T," Col. Hadley, page 62.

laundry, food and packing houses, the needle trades, painters, furniture workers, miners, railroad workers, rubber and textile workers, leather workers, etc. Then we find the United Farmers' League, the American Negro Labor Congress, Workers of Library Publishers, Council for Working Class Women, Bezboshnik (Russian godless society), Labor Sports Union, Young Communist League, Young Pioneers of America, Negro Champion, Young Comrade, International Press, Friends of the Soviet Union (with modernistic preachers and educators as paying members), Hungarian Sick and Benefit Society, etc., etc.

Still more astonishing is the communistic press. It has a paid circulation of about 350,000. One of the leading papers is the "Daily Worker." In ten months it doubled its subscription list. Its issues, it is said, are from 35,000 to 40,000 copies. Other English periodicals are: "Labor Defender," "Young Worker," "United Farmer," "Labor Unity," "Working Women," "Southern Worker," "Communist," "Liberator" and others. Other periodicals are published in Yiddish, Russian, Polish, Finnish, Italian, Scandinavian, Greek, Lithuanian, Bohemian, German, Armenian, Bulgarian, Lettish, Estonian and Japanese. We recommend our interested readers to study Report 2290 of the Seventy-first Congress published in 1931 to see what Communism has achieved in the line of organization and publicity during the few years of its existence.

Perhaps the most serious aspect of this un-American propaganda, aiming at the destruction of our American ideals and institutions, besides all religion, is its activity among the young people. The communists conduct an extensive and intensive campaign among the young for the spread of the communistic doctrines, attempting to prepare them for militant participation and leadership in the future revolution, when the bloody scenes of Russia of 1917-1920 are to be repeated. The "Young Pioneers of America" and the "Young Communist League" are imitations of the Boy Scouts of America. They are both dedicated to the hatred of American institutions and the American flag.

They are stirred up in every possible way to wage a relentless warfare against all religious beliefs and to hold their own parents in contempt and disobey them in case they maintain faith in God. It is not enough that they are irreligious, but they must be anti-religious. Then there are communist summer schools and camps. Here the most pernicious work is done. These schools are in different parts of the country. In the state of New York yearly 15,000 young communists are turned out with intense class hatred, as well as hatred of God, hatred of our government and hatred of American traditions. The Fish Congressional Report says: "In the vicinity of New York City the Communist camps include a *very high percentage of Jewish boys and girls, estimated to be as high as ninety per cent**. There is no Federal law prohibiting such camps teaching disloyalty and practically treason to thousands of healthy and bright young future Americans, and they are permitted to exist and continue to warp the minds of immature children whose parents have fled from countries where they were oppressed to a land of freedom and equal opportunity."†

During May, 1933, in *Amherst College*, where certain teachers may have spread the seed of infidelity, a score of freshmen burned the American flag in a Communist demonstration. They call themselves "the sincere Communists of Amherst College." They sang the Internationale. The newspaper report said that the president, Dr. Stanley King, *"declined to comment on the incident."* In 1929 a "Children's Congress" was held in Moscow. Seven boys and girls, about the age of fourteen, were sent from the United States as delegates, among them a young negro, who had left the Boy Scouts and joined the Pioneers. One of the delegates, a vicious youngster, was arrested before the departure of the delegation. After these delegates returned they became

---

*As we write this a High School teacher sent a letter requesting information as to the "Young Pioneers." This teacher has a large number of Jewish children who are "Pioneers" and they are making efforts to spread their revolutionary propaganda among others.

†Congressional Report, page 28.

very active among school children.   One young girl, daughter
of foreign-born parents, concluded her speeches: "Remember the only country we have is Soviet Russia—we children
of today will be the leaders of the revolutionary movement
a few years hence, when we will make this country another
Russia."

They have now also established "Communist-Workers
Schools."   They are in existence in New York, Chicago,
Detroit, Los Angeles, Cleveland, Seattle, Portland, Oregon,
Youngstown, Pontiac and other places.   Here revolution
against the American government, the tactics of revolution
and probably the different forms of violence, besides hatred
of religion, are systematically taught.   And here again
our government is still asleep.

Another activity is among the negro residents.   In order
to give facts to the reader who has not access to the Congressional Report, we quote from it.*

"The communists for years have looked hopefully toward the negro
residents of the United States as an element where they might gain
recruits for the Communist Party.   Work among the negroes is con-
sidered one of the major activities of the party.

"Up until this time, the communist effort to interest and line up the
negroes in this country has not met with great success, although a
considerable number of negroes employed in the northern industrial
centers have joined the movement.   In the South efforts among the
negroes have not been very fruitful, although some headway has been
made in certain sections.

"The Communist Party has a negro work department and a national
negro organizer.   This special department extends down through all
communist units, including the District, the section, and finally to
each unit or nucleus, with a responsible director.

"The task of the communists among the negro workers is to bring
about class consciousness, and to crystallize this in independent class
political action against the capitalist class; to take every possible
advantage of occurrences and conditions which will tend to develop
race feeling with the view of utilizing racial antagonism.   At every
opportunity the attempt is made to stir up trouble between the white
and negro races.

"The negroes are made to believe that the communists practice complete racial and social equality and that only when a communist

---

*Congressional Report, pages 32-33.

Government is set up in the United States will the negroes obtain equality and freedom from exploitation by the 'white bosses, and in order to attract and impress the negro, the communists make a point of encouraging mixed social functions where white women communists dance with negro men and white men communists dance with negro women. It is openly advocated that there must be complete social and racial equality between the whites and negroes even to the extent of intermarriage.

Several pages in the Congressional Report are devoted to the propaganda which is carried on in our military organizations—the Army, the National Guard, the military training camps and units in schools and colleges. Young Communists sneak in, enlist and then carry on an underhanded work to create a revolutionary spirit. A small sheet, "The Rebel Guard," is published by them and secretly circulated. They attempt to break down the morale of our defense forces and also try to discourage enlistments. In connection with the schools, colleges and universities, the report says: "The evidence presented to the committee of communist attacks against military training in schools and colleges is extensive. Such activities have led to considerable agitation in some of the big universities. Opposition to military training in educational institutions provides a fertile field for inflammatory speeches and articles by young communists who pose as favoring eternal peace while advocating civil war and revolution." Let it be remembered that Professor Einstein, the socialist and scientist, sent a telegram after his first visit to our hospitable shores, to a large gathering of young people's societies, advising them to become "militant pacifists." Of late, we believe, he has taken a more positive stand and has become the president of some youth pacific organization. A high official of the United States, who knows what he is talking about, said:

"It is well to remember that the political power in control of Russia has declared war on the United States, and is today openly advocating the overthrow of this government in every place and at every opportunity. Russia evidently is preparing to fight the world. Preaching disarmament among other nations, she is today creating the greatest war machine the world has ever known.

"We will face a new alignment in the next war. We will forget our foes of the World War and welcome them as allies. This is not an alarmist theory. Foes of the recent conflict will work together against the common enemy for the preservation of our government, our homes and firesides, and our religion, for we face the loss of all these if any enemy bent on their wholesale destruction should triumph."

And this destructive propaganda continues, as we prove later, by a certain class of American educators and the so-called "men of the cloth," clergymen of different denominations.

Congressman John E. Nelson made some statements which present the situation in the right light:

"Communism in the United States is organized on the theories of Karl Marx, with tactics applied by Nicholas Lenin. Their objectives are definite and they have adopted an uncompromising policy by which to attain them. The postulates of American communism, openly declared, are as follows:

To arouse working-class consciousness.
To teach that our Government is dominated and controlled by and for the capitalist class; that the workers "produce everything and own nothing," and the capitalists "produce nothing and own everything."
To educate the masses to a common view point, and set them up as enemies of capitalistic society.
To prepare them for the revolution that is to usher in the dictatorship of the proletariat.
To expropriate all means and instrumentalities of production, and to suppress or eliminate all those who may oppose them.
To make America a Soviet Republic.

"The idea that all American communists are ignorant rogues and selfish adventurers must be dismissed, if we are to have a proper conception of this communist situation. The actual dues-paying members of the Communist Party in the United States are, as a rule, men and women of foreign extraction, of unusual intelligence and ability, actuated by no hope of personal reward, and absolutely devoted to their cause, for which they are ever ready to sacrifice their time, health, and talents. They are the heralds of a new social philosophy, the apostles of an intellectual religion divorced of all spirituality, and the captains of an army. Absolute obedience and continual activity are demanded of every member and they are subject to a discipline as exacting as that of any military organization. The communist is a zealot, supremely self-confident, and as devoid of compassion as an executioner. Whether we like it or not, theirs is the old crusader spirit, modernized with the instruments and methods of today. All this gives them a strength and influence all out of proportion to their numbers, a kind of strength possessed, perhaps by no other organization in this country."

He also states the fact that orders for work, the work of destroying our country are received directly from Moscow. Groups of workers, including negroes and young people of both sexes, are continually sent to Russia to be trained as communist agitators and active revolutionists. They are ordered to bore from within, in the army, the navy, the national guard, the schools, the labor unions, the industries, the American Legion, and to establish themselves in key positions, to be ready for leadership when the day of revolution comes.

One of the chief aims of this vicious propaganda is to overthrow the "American Federation of Labor." If this were achieved the doom of this country would have arrived. The late Samuel Gompers, a patriotic American citizen opposed these agitations and so do also the present excellent leaders of the Federation, Mr. Green and the Vice-President Matthew Woll.

And how many pages might be filled with the commercial aspect, the never-ceasing attempts to hurt our commercial enterprises and industries by "dumping". Russia itself is agriculturally and also industrially in a desperate condition. To give just a faint glimpse of what has happened and the misery, which exists in that land of godlessness, we quote from Report 2290 of the Seventy-first Congress:

"The Communist Party in Russia consists very largely of members from the industrial centers, and is directed by city workers for their own benefit. The peasants were looked down on as inferior beings and were regarded as little better than animals to plant and harvest the food supply for the city workers. Consequently there was no cooperation between the communist city workers and the peasants, and the bulk of the peasants hated and feared the communists, who sent out expeditions into the farming country and confiscated most of the grain from the farmers on various pretexts, such as nonpayment of taxes or counter revolution, or paid for it in worthless currency or receipts for government bonds. The poor peasant became more and more exasperated and often found the more he harvested the less he had, so he began to plant only a sufficient amount for the needs of his own family. The result was in effect a gigantic, though undirected, strike by the peasants of Russia, which forced the Soviet Government to change its tactics. First it permitted a modified free trade and agriculture revived. Lately it has begun to create huge state farms and organize the peasants into enormous producing cooperatives.

The first step was a campaign to eliminate or liquidate the Kulaks, or so-called rich farmers, who were bitterly opposed to communism. These Kulaks were the more thrifty farmers who were able, through individual effort, to acquire a few cows and horses and live in a better house than the other peasants. These Kulaks were not rich in the sense of American farmers, as they probably did not make over a couple of hundred dollars a year, yet the word went out from Moscow that they must be suppressed. A reign of terror ensued. Peasants were told that they could take away the property of any Kulak who had as much as two cows or two horses and the red army and police were used to wipe out the Kulaks. In turn these farmers, the best in Russia, began in desperation to kill off their cattle, so that in 1928-29 it is estimated that 15,000,000 head of cattle were slaughtered, seriously impairing the milk, butter, and cheese supply of Russia, and also the production of beef.

"It is difficult to ascertain accurate figures as to the number of Kulaks that were driven out of their homes and deported to the northern forests to cut timber or to work on the roads in Siberia. *The figures available vary all the way from 500,000 to 5,000,000, and the truth is probably about halfway between.* The suffering that these Kulaks endured, together with their families, is one of the terrible tragedies of recent Russian history.

"The ruthlessness of the Soviet Government in liquidating the Kulaks aroused the sympathy of the peasants and caused widespread resistance and antagonism so that Stalin issued an edict from Moscow that the Kulak liquidation had gone far enough and that from now on only counter-revolutionists among the peasants would be suppressed. The warfare against the Kulaks had brought about chaos in Russian agriculture, as the best farmers and those who gave employment had been deported or ruined.

We must refrain from mentioning other different forms

of the Russian propaganda and such organizations as the "United Farmers' League" with headquarters in Minnesota, spreading Communism throughout the Northwest and sowing the seed of revolution; the "All American Imperialistic League" which aims at the rebellion of Mexico and South America against the United States. There is also a certain "Press Federation" which is serving Communism; the "League for Industrial Democracy," a radical organization active in universities and colleges disseminating its theories among our American youth through liberal clubs; "The Friends of the Soviet Union," raising money to promote friendly relations with Russia, aiming at recognition; "*International Labor Defense*," which is a branch of the International Red Aid of Moscow. This labor defense spreads communistic propaganda through the publicity derived from the radical, so-called class-war prisoners. It claims to defend all workers who are being persecuted by "the capitalistic government." These prisoners, who have been guilty of criminal actions, receive through this labor defense, bail bonds, attorneys' fees, etc. For instance, the Sacco-Vanizetti case, the Mooney-Billings case, the Gastonia case and others were carried on by this defense. In the case of the defendants tried for killing the police chief of Gastonia, about $30,000 was furnished by the Garland fund and the communistic organizations in our land gave $100,000. Yet not a dollar came into the hands of the men conducting the defense. The Garland fund has kept this labor defense and also the "American Civil Liberties Union," of which we shall have more to say, partly in funds.

The field of their greatest activities has been the different industries where they have fomented discontent, which has led to serious strikes. Underneath is a most pernicious propaganda. While they demand certain concessions and reforms they maliciously obstruct and prevent their execution. The leading communistic-led strikes took place among the textile workers in Paterson, N. J. The leaders were, to judge by their names, foreigners—Weisbrod, Rubenstein, Wagenknecht and others. Then came strikes among the fur workers of New York, in Bedford, Massachusetts, in Gastonia, South Carolina, where the chief of police was murdered, a shoe strike in New York City. Many other strikes were engineered by them, among the dental workers, the needle trade, the window cleaners and cafeteria workers.

There is an organization in this country, which has been a great encouragement to this foreign and revolutionary element. It is the Red-defending "American Civil Liberties Union." As the real character of this organization is not generally known, we quote what the Congressional Investigation Committee has to say about them. (Report 2290, p. 52.)

"The American Civil Liberties Union is closely affiliated with the communist movement in the United States, and fully 90 per cent of its efforts are on behalf of communists who have come into conflict with the law. It claims to stand for free speech, free press, and free assembly; but it is quite apparent that the main function of the A. C. L. U. is to attempt to protect the communists in their advocacy of force and violence to overthrow the Government, replacing the American flag by a red flag and erecting a Soviet Government in place of the republican form of government guaranteed to each State by the Federal Constitution.

"Roger N. Baldwin, its guiding spirit, makes no attempt to hide his friendship for the communists and their principles. He was formerly a member of the I. W. W. and served a term in prison as a draft dodger during the war. This is the same Roger N. Baldwin that has recently issued a statement 'that in the next session of Congress our job is to organize the opposition to the recommendations of the congressional committee investigating communism.' In his testimony before the committee he admitted having said at a dinner held in Chicago that 'The Fish Committee recommendation will be buried in the Senate.' Testifying on force and violence, murder, etc., the following is quoted:

The CHAIRMAN. Does your organization uphold the right of a citizen or alien—it does not make any difference which—to advocate murder?
Mr. BALDWIN. Yes.
The CHAIRMAN. Or assassination?
Mr. BALDWIN. Yes.
The CHAIRMAN. Does your organization uphold the right of an

American citizen to advocate force and violence for the overthrow of the Government.

Mr. BALDWIN. Certainly; in so far as mere advocacy is concerned.

The CHAIRMAN. Does it uphold the right of an alien in this country to urge the overthrow and advocate the overthrow of the Government by force and violence?

Mr. BALDWIN. Precisely on the same basis as any citizen.

The CHAIRMAN. You do uphold the right of an alien to advocate the overthrow of the Government by force and violence?

Mr. BALDWIN. Sure; certainly. It is the healthiest kind of thing for a country, of course, to have free speech—unlimited.

"The American Civil Liberties Union has received large sums from the Garland fund, of which Roger N. Baldwin is one of the directors. During the trial of the communists at Gastonia, not for freedom of speech, of the press, or assembly, but for a conspiracy to kill the chief of police, of which seven defendants were convicted, the A. C. L. U. provided bail for five of the defendants, amounting to $28,500, which it secured from the Garland fund. All of the defendants convicted jumped their bail and are reported to be in Russia. The $28,500 bail was forfeited, including $9,000 more advanced by the International Labor Defense.

"A committee of the New York State Legislature, back in 1928, reached the following conclusion in regard to the American Civil Liberties Union:

The American Civil Liberties Union, in the last analysis, is a supporter of all subversive movements; its propaganda is detrimental to the interests of the State. It attempts not only to protect crime but to encourage attacks upon our institutions in every form.

"Your committee concurs with the above findings.

"The principles of free speech, free press, and free assembly are worthy of an organization that stands for our republican form of government, guaranteed by the Constitution, and for the ideals of Washington, Jefferson, and Lincoln, instead of an organization whose main work is to uphold the communists in spreading revolutionary propaganda and inciting revolutionary activities to undermine our American institutions and overthrow our Federal Government."

In the membership of this Red-defending organization we find a strange combination. Here are out and out atheists, free-thinkers, agnostics, politicians, preachers of different evangelical denominations, editors of "religious periodicals," and professors in various institutions of learning including theological seminaries. How can Communism with its agitation against government, private

ownership, above all *against God and against His Christ,
against religion and against the church,* this menace of our
country, be curtailed if "Christian" preachers and educators
help along its continuance? Here is an item which should
open the eyes of every reader.

"More than four hundred educators and clergymen of the
'liberal' and radical type have signed a memorial in favor
of the removal by Congress of the U. S. Treasury's right to
exclude from entry at the customs houses obscene books,
pamphlets and circulars. One of the signers of this memorial
is Bishop Francis McConnell, president of the Federal Council
of Churches of Christ. Another is Rev. Harry F. Ward,
of Union Theological Seminary, president of the American
Civil Liberties Union. The circulation of most of the
material thus excluded by the Treasury is criminal under
Federal and state laws; the effect of removing the Treasury
restrictions would be, however, to make its access to the
country easier. Bootlegging this obscenity is one of the
active New York 'rackets.' Some of the material already
excluded by the Treasury specifically mentioned in the Senate
debate as representing unwise 'censorship,' is of the pervert
and degenerate type. The worst of this type of European
'literary' filth has not heretofore even been offered for entry
into this country, because of the restriction it is now proposed
to strike down. Some of it is obscene attack on religious
faith."*

The same issue of the "*National Republic*" shows where
Harry E. Fosdick of the Riverside Church, New York City,
stands, and he has thousands of followers among the "clergy"
and men and women in cap and gown.

"It has often been stated in these columns that among
the most active apologists for Soviet Russia in the United
States are ministers of radical and 'liberal' affiliations.
Eighty-seven ministers, headed by Harry Emerson Fosdick,
on March 6 issued a statement deprecating the absence of a
'note of humility' in Christian and Jewish protests against
the slaughter, jailing and general repression of religious
workers in Russia, and declaring that the anti-religious
atttiude of communism is due 'to the failure of the churches
to recognize their obligations to the social and economic
needs of the people.' The statement argued that 'whatever

*National Republic, April, 1930, page 36.

values may be born out of the Russian experiment should be given the opportunity to mature' and an appreciation of all efforts to 'bring about a closer understanding between the Russian people and the outside world' was urged. 'An adequate commission of research and inquiry' was suggested. The claim that the atheism of Soviet Russia is due to the character of the Green Orthodox Church of course no longer has weight, in view of the fact that in their campaign for the extermination of religion, the Moscow masters now frankly extend their system of terrorism and repression to all forms of religion. Atheism is fundamental in communism as is the system of extirpating by terrorism all opinions, either religious or economic, not in accord with communist doctrines. The proposal of compromise and understanding with such a system and the suggestion of any value or virtue in it, coming from a quarter long known to be tolerant if not sympathetic with bolshevism, is grotesque. Reformists and socialists of the type joining in this ministerial outgiving are today the most hated targets of bolshevist persecution and if, on Russian soil, they were to criticize the soviet government as freely as most of them habitiually do the American government, they would have to finish the argument in front of a firing squad.''

To show the utter blindness of these religious leaders we quote from the February issue (1930) of the "Federal Council Bulletin" of the Federal Council of Churches, of which the modernistic methodist *Bishop Francis McConnell* used to be president. In an article by a Rev. O. J. Price we read:

"These two views of life (i. e., the Christian and the communist) have much in common—both are seeking the salvation of humanity, both are international in outlook and both create and secure supreme personal loyalty and sacrifice."

What a slander of Christianity, which does not seek the salvation of humanity, but offers salvation in Christ. Nor does Communism have anything to offer but destruction in its program.

Frequently protests are made against police action in dealing with the riotous Communists. Among these protesters we find Dr. Henry Sloane Coffin, President of the Union Theological Seminary, Professor and Mrs. Charles

A. Beard, Professor John Dewey of Columbia, Susan Brandeis, daughter of Supreme Court Justice Brandeis, and others.

Several years ago the "*New York Herald Tribune*" published a most enlightening article on the changing religious views during the last fifty years. We reproduce a paragraph, quoted by the writer in his magazine, "Our Hope":

"The arrest of a flock of students from the Union Theological Seminary for picketing in the recent dressmakers' strike might cause the visitor to make inquiries, and he would find that there was a definite trend among students for the ministry and young clergymen toward making the church a sociological institution; that many of them were getting their doctrines from the writings of social reformers, from the British Labor Party and from *Soviet teaching* rather than from books of theology. He would learn that the intellectual leaders among the young clergy criticized the church as a reactionary middle class institution; that they regarded the ideas of the saving of souls and of the reward in the hereafter as relics of days of unenlightenment, and that it was their program to direct the energy and devotion and emotional enthusiasm of religious men and women toward the solution of the industrial, social and racial problems of the present day. He would find young clergymen here and there engaged in such enterprises as organizing strikes or inducing the white members of the parish to mingle socially at dances and card parties with their Negro co-religionists."

Let us remember that Dr. Henry Sloane Coffin is the President of the "Seminary" and one of the professors is Dr. Harry Emerson Fosdick, who has plastered on his church-building the figures of Darwin and Einstein. This institution has rejected supernatural Christianity. Here we must mention two preachers of the modernistic type, who went to Russia on invitation of their friends, the Soviets. They were well guarded and were led only to places where they saw certain things, the horrible miseries of the enslaved millions were kept in the back ground. Returning one of these men spoke in the "Clergy Club" of New York City and is reported to have said, "These Russian Soviets, though they are atheistic, succeed better in putting the kingdom of God on earth than we do with all our churches in America." Legislation has been brought about to deport aliens who are caught in anti-government activities. The bill should include "clergymen" who are dissatisfied with our country, who lend a hand in the attempted overthrow of our institutions. Put them on a ship and send them to Russia to help them build "the kingdom of God" over there!

About a year ago there was held in the same New York Seminary the "New York Intercollegiate Conference." The program covered several days. The two leading topics under discussion were "Guiding the Revolution" and "New Tactics in the Social Conflict." One of the leading speakers was Norman Thomas, a former student of this Seminary, one time a Presbyterian preacher, now Socialist of the outspoken kind. Many colleges and universities were represented. Speeches were made on themes like these: "Students and the World Revolution," "Revolution Through Education," "The American Civil War of 1931-32." Then arrived a telegram from the all-red Chicago Conference for the League of Industrial Democracy, greeting the Theological Seminary Conference—it read: "Swell Conference. Twenty-three colleges represented. *Yours for the revolution.*"

And there are ostrich congressmen and senators who laughingly say—no danger!

A certain New York-modernistic-pacifistic pastor, who also had visited Russia, preached on "If I Were a Dictator." Here is his answer: "I would close the Churches, abolish tariff-walls, eliminate armaments, teach birth control in the public schools and make a knowledge of contraceptive methods a legal prerequisite to marriage." He also said: "No one institution has so blocked the progress of modern civilization as the Church. Empires come and go, but the Church stays on forever."

One of the prominent religious organizations, seems to be the "*Methodist Federation for Social Service.*" This organization is committed to the Socialistic propaganda. Its leading spirit is the Rev. Harry F. Ward. He is radical and closely identified with the "American Civil Liberties Union." This Methodist Preacher says in his book, "The New Social Order," that the system under which our Government is living is doomed to go, and whether or not the new order comes peacably, or through violence depends on the so-called middle and property class (the bourgeoisie). This class, according to Ward, must bow to the inevitable and allow the proletariat of the world to establish the new social order for which these men are working, or a violent revolution will follow. Mr. Ward is an ardent exponent of Syndicalism. The *National Republic*, February 1932, in an article by George B. Lockwood says: "Harry F. Ward, head of the Methodist Federation for Social Service, now in Moscow, drinking deep from the head-springs of Bolshevism, has been active as a director of the American Civil Liberties Union. On this Board he sat alongside some of the Communist leaders of the country. He was a delegate to the Anti-Imperialistic League held in Frankfurt, the organization which is a subsidiary of the third internationale. He is also a professor in the Union Theological Seminary."

And so we could continue filling page after page with the ever increasing undermining propaganda which is done by some preachers and teachers in colleges. They are strengthening the hands of Stalin whose acts of violence, cruelty and inhumanity are beginning to overshadow the deeds of Lenin and Trotzsky-Bronstein.

We don't know how many of these baptized "comrades" bow before the edict of the red dictator, but they are certainly working in harmony with his schemes.

We must mention another bulletin of the "Methodist Federation," Bulletin No. 8, published April 15, 1932:

"In this bulletin is found an acknowledgment over the signatures of Bishop Francis J. McConnell, President, and Harry F. Ward, Secretary for the Federation, that, 'The Federation has continued to co-operate with boards and agencies within our own church and with *many groups outside the church* working definitely for a *new social order.* Among these may be mentioned the *American Civil Liberties*

Union, the League of Industrial Democracy, Labor Research Association, International Labor Defense, Committee on Militarism in Education, Fellowship of Reconciliation . . .'

"Bishop McConnell says in the Bulletin, *'We simply cannot be respectable—.* These questions we raise in our Bulletin simply have to be got up for consideration in religious circles. *We can't be bothered to discuss what everyone else is discussing.* We must go ahead and *raise other questions.'* "

Note the affiliation with the organizations which have been unmasked in their socialistic-communistic propaganda. The "new social order" for which this Methodist Bishop is working can mean nothing else but that for which these radical organizations stand. We give a little more light on some of these organizations.

The Fellowship of Reconciliation is an organization which, according to the history of its movement, devoted its time in the United States during the World War period to "defending conscientious objectors and opposing war propaganda" while the government was making desperate efforts to mobilize. The members of this latter organization are responsible for the creation of Brookwood Labor College, a socialist center, and for Reconciliation Tours, operating in New York City for the purpose of taking excursions of students into the haunts of communism, I. W. W.'ism, birth control, atheism and other subversive movements. The Committee on Militarism in Education, another of the Methodist bureau's "co-operating" organizations, according to the history of the Fellowship of Reconciliation, was set up by it, although most of its officials are from the ranks of the American Civil Liberties Union. The Labor Research Association, still another Methodist bureau co-operating organization, is a fountain head for much radical literature.

And all along while men of the stamp of Sherwood Eddy, once a Gospel preacher and Y. M. C. A. worker, but now a Socialist, and professors of the Union Seminary, paint rosy pictures of the red Republic, returning Americans, who lived in Russia, tell a different story.

"The wife of another American engineer, Mrs. MacMurray, came back a few weeks ago. 'I'll never go back,' she said. 'Sorrow, fear and hate, combined with a jeering contempt for the finer things of life, hang over the land of the Soviets.' Then she declared: 'No moral code is preserved. Men and women live together like animals. They live where and how the Government directs. All labor is forced labor. If they do not work where the Government commands, they are refused a food card. I could not make friends. The people are afraid of everyone and of everything.'

"Such is the Red Paradise!"

But this is almost unbelievable—an infidel, once professor in a certain college, where he taught his infidelity, also a member of the different socialistic-communistic organizations, said: "Communism is the great secular religion with Marx in the place of Jehovah, Lenin in the place of Jesus, Trotzsky in the place of St. Paul and Stalin in the place of St. Peter." Here the coming man of sin, the beast, shows its teeth.

The agitation for the "new social order" à la Russia evidently is everywhere. The August issue (1932) of the "National Republic" reports the following:

"Dr. Albert E. Taussig of Washington University, St. Louis, Missouri, has accepted the presidency of the St. Louis branch of the red defending American Civil Liberties Union. Rev. George M. Gibson, Rabbi Isserman, Bishop William Scarlett of the Protestant Episcopal Church, Prof. George Stephens, Dean Sidney Sweet, Rev. Ralph Abele and Professor Fuchs accepted the directorship of the radical organization."

The same Monthly tells its readers in the December issue (1932):

"Many strange bedfellows were found with the revolutionary elements of the country during the recent election campaign. Among the ministers that were finally forced to come out in the open in their activities in behalf of red candidates for President and Vice-President of the United States were: Bishop Francis J. McConnell, of the Methodist Federation for Social Service and President of the Federal Council of Churches, who helped organize the nation for the Socialist candidate for President and Vice-President; Rev. Allan Knight Chalmers, pastor of the Broadway Congregational Tabernacle of New York City; Rev. John Haynes Holmes of New York City, prominent in red circles; Reverends Charles C. Noble, Eugene Schrigler,

A. Raymond Grant, Walter Foley, John C. Vernon, Carl Clark, John K.
Montgomery, J. Lester Hawkins, C. H. Davis, Glen Trimble, O. B.
Wells, Donald H. Tippett, Robert J. Tucker, Fred W. Adams, Frank
Kingdon, Halford Luccock, Edgar S. Brightman, Irving Beiler, Paul
Hutchinson, Dan B. Brummitt, Harold W. Ruopp, Howard H.
Callaghan, while Winifred Chappell of the Methodist Federation for
Social Service was among those who helped organize the nation for
the communist candidates, Foster and Ford."

The question arises, how can this strange fact, that preachers and educators, who claim to be Christians, are active
in this propaganda, be explained? How can it be explained
that these men, who profess to be religious, can link themselves to the communistic idea and work for it, when Communism is anti-God, anti-religion, anti-Christ, and anti-
Church?

Has Communism changed? NO! It still stands firmly
by Lenin and his Satanic saying: "Religion is the opium
of the people. We must fight against religion. We must
create a militant atheism." The Third Internationale
still demands that its law is obeyed—"Among the objectives
of the cultural revolution interesting the great mass of the
population, the struggle against religion, that opium of the
people, holds a special place; this struggle must be carried
on inflexibly and systematically." They have not changed.
The five-year plan of the godless, the "*Bezbojnik*," is the
practical evidence that there has not been a change. But
how can it be explained?

The answer is very simple. We give six words and these
six words contain the answer: *Bible Criticism—Modernistic
Apostasy, Atheism—Socialism—Communism, Ruin*. These
words are the horrible steps taken by these present-day
leaders and educators of Christendom. It is the fulfilment
of Bible predictions, we quoted before, which nineteen hundred years ago were written by the Spirit of God as a warning of what the end of Christendom would be. First the
Bible as God's Word and revelation is rejected. It begins
in a small way. The authorship of the Pentateuch by
Moses is questioned. The opening chapters of Genesis
are mythological conceptions handed down by the Hebrews.

Direct Creation is questioned and next they cast themselves into the fogs of evolution, believing, as we have shown in our opening chapter, that the foolish inventions of Charles Darwin and others, are the real solution of human existence. Then they go step by step towards a total rejection of the Bible as the supernatural Book of God. Out of this comes the religious modernism, which is apostasy from the faith. Religious modernism, like its author, the power which controls it, the father of lies, does nothing but negate.

Can the Bible be trusted as being the supernatural revelation of God? The religious modernism answers decisively— No! Is Christ the eternal Son of God? Another—No! He was a good man, a religious leader on the same level with Buddha Gautama, Zoroaster and Confucius. They go a step further and claim Him to have been a Socialist and several years ago a Presbyterian preacher, perhaps a product of the Union Theological Seminary, declared that Christ was a Communist and if he came back to the world and would teach again, they would deport him. Let us remind ourselves that such claims, as Christ being a Socialist, stated in a previous chapter, were also made by the infidel followers of Illuminism during the nineteenth century. Was Christ born of the Virgin? No! Biology cannot explain such an occurrence. But biology is unable to explain many other facts and the questions we like to have answered remain for ever unanswered. Did He die a sacrificial death for our sins? The evolution theory does not believe in the fall of man. Sin, as it is spoken of in the Scriptures, does not exist. Atonement, they say, is a theological invention. He died for the socialistic principles He advocated, as a martyr. He was buried—was He raised from among the dead? Dr. Harry E. Fosdick has been reported as saying: "His body rests in a Syrian grave, but His soul is marching on." With the denial of the physical resurrection of Jesus Christ, Christianity collapses and becomes a religious system without power, without hope—and worse, a system of deception and delusion (1 Cor. xv:13-19). Yet many hundreds of Methodist, Baptist,

Presbyterian, Congregational, Episcopal preachers and educators and those of other denominations, brazenly deny this cardinal truth of Christianity. And because they believe that Christ died, as others die, and that of His body it is true, "dust to dust, ashes to ashes," they reject His priesthood. The Person of Christ is non-existent; He only lives by His example, His words and His teachings. Then they become "Agnostics" (in Latin: *Ignoramus*)—know-nothings—free-thinkers, atheists. Dr. Harry E. Fosdick is quoted as having said in a sermon: "You may be surprised when I, a minister, say to you that it does not matter very much whether you believe in God or not." Professor W. N. Weiman of the *Divinity* School, Chicago University, wrote: "In what sense (i. e., the Divine Being) may be called personal is a matter of further consideration. With me it is an open question whether God is a personal Being, a thing, or a principle."

And here is Dr. Shailer Matthews in his "The Growth of the Idea of God," published in 1931. He is the head of this so-called "Divinity School." In this book he repudiates the idea of God as a Sovereign, also the doctrine that God is a spirit. He also denies the existence of the soul.* These modern apostates, whose constant increase is fostered by these infidel, dishonest institutions, which sail under the name of Christianity, but are in reality the destroyers of the foundations of righteousness open wide the gates for our youth into the hell of atheism.

Having become infidels by rejecting God's holy Word, God's holy Son and God's holy Gospel, the one power in the world, which can save man and lead him to righteousness and peace, they turn to Socialism, to Communism as the saviours of humanity. How true it is which was spoken by the lips of the Son of God: "If therefore the light which is in thee become darkness, how great is that darkness!" (Matt. vi:23). What they are coming to may be learned from a publication in connection with the Union Theological Seminary. In *"Religion Today,"* a symposium on the

*"God and Cosmos," Dr. Graebner, page 21.

question "the future of the Church," was recently printed. A certain "reverend," who is radical, expressed himself as follows:

"There will be no gods in the future, no Jehovah and no Lord, but to quote the words of Charles W. Eliot—one omnipresent, eternal energy, informing and inspiring the whole creation at any instant of time and throughout indefinite spaces. There will be no churches as we have churches today. There will be just the community, with its sacred places of the common life. An hour each day will be given to communal consecration and will replace Sunday. Bibles will be replaced by the assembled literature of all ages and peoples, the works of universal genius sanctified by usage, and growing with the growing vision of men's minds and hearts. There will be a new calendar of saints, including Jesus, Isaiah, George Fox, Darwin, Pasteur, Lincoln, Emerson, Tolstoy and Gandhi."

The "American Association for the Advancement of Atheism" and "Freethinkers' Association" were right when they called these "Reverends" "brothers" and invited them to join in with them and assist in the work of destruction.

That able theologian, scholar and president of Princeton, the late Dr. Francis L. Patton, spoke a number of years ago words of tremendous importance and significance: **"The only hope of Christianity is in the rehabilitating of the Pauline theology. It is back, back, back to an incarnate Christ and the atoning blood, or it is on, on, on to atheism and despair."**

These are golden words. The road of modernism, including the "famous" middle-of-the-roaders, who are neither fish nor fowl, who are trembling lest they might lose position and popularity,—this road leads, on, on, on to atheism, to world revolution, national disaster and finally to the judgment of Almighty God.

Can America be saved from such a horrible goal? **YES.** But salvation can come only by a whole-hearted return to God, by confession of sins and repentance, by a renewed preaching of the Gospel of God, the power of God unto salvation. Let the hopeless apostates, who have turned away from the Christ of God and become advocates of the destructive forces of the mystery of lawlessness, let them follow their road.   Long ago their coming doom was written in the Word of God—"*their end is destruction*" (Phil. iii:19). But let the millions who still maintain faith in God and in His Word (though many hundreds of thousands in profession only), let them turn to the Lord in humiliation.   Let true believers yield themselves fully to the Lord and give an outspoken witness for Him.   The Lord can answer by the manifestation of His Spirit in sending such a powerful revival, which will be God's answer to the prevailing infidelity.

History reveals the fact that while France suffered untold horrors in the revolution during the closing years of the eighteenth century, England escaped.   Edward Hartpole Lecky in his comprehensive "History of England," devotes a good deal of space to the moral conditions in England. He also mentions in a number of pages the great religious revivals under the Wesleys, George Whitefield and others. More than that, he shows that these revivals saved England from the fate of the bloody revolution through which France was passing.   We quote his words which are well worth reading.

"Before the close of the century in which the Evangelical revival appeared, a spirit had begun to circulate in Europe threatening the very foundations of society and of belief.   The revolt against the supernatural theory of Christianity, which had been conducted by Voltaire and the Encyclopaedists, the material conception of man and of the universe, which sprang from the increased study of physical science and from the metaphysics of Condillac and Helvetius, the wild social dreams which Rousseau had clothed in such a transcendent eloquence, the misery of a high-spirited people ground to the dust by unnecessary wars and by partial and unjust taxation, the imbecility and corruption of rulers and priests, had together produced in France a revolutionary spirit, which in its intensity was unequalled since the days of the Reformation.   It was soon felt in many lands.   Millions of fierce and ardent natures were intoxicated by dreams of an impossible equality and of a complete social and political reorganization.   Many old excuses perished, but a tone of thought and feeling was introduced into European life which could only lead to Anarchy, and at length to despotism, and was beyond all others fatal to that measured and ordered freedom which can only endure.   Its chief characteristics were, a hatred of all constituted authority, an insatiable appetite for change, a habit of regarding rebellion as the normal as well as the noblest form of political self-sacrifice, a disdain for all compromise, a contempt for all tradition, a desire to level all ranks and subvert all establishments, a determination to seek progress, not by the slow and cautious amelioration of existing institutions, but by sudden, violent, and revolutionary change. Religion, property, civil authority, and domestic life, were all assailed and doctrines incompatible with the very existence of government were embraced by multitudes with the fervor of religion. England, on the whole, escaped the contagion. Many causes conspired to save her, but among them a prominent place must, I believe, be given to the new and vehement religious enthusiasm which was at that very time passing through the middle and lower classes of people, which had enlisted in its service a large proportion of the wilder and more impetuous reformers, and which recoiled with horror from the anti-Christian tenets that were associated with the Revolution in France."

And *if* there is no return to God, if there is no genuine repentance, if Christendom continues in its downward grade, in its Satanic denials, in its road of Christ rejection and atheism—*then what?* History repeats itself. Once upon a time there existed great churches in northern Egypt and northern Africa, in Asia Minor, also in eastern Europe. But they had gone into apostasy. As a result all forms of unrighteousness and licentiousness followed. Then when the measure was full God permitted the rise of Mohammedanism and used the hordes of Arabia to wipe out that apostate Christian civilization. And if modernism continues without repentance and in its denials, then God will permit the Russian *"hammer"* to demolish our country, and the Russian *"sickle"* to reap a greater and more bloody harvest than the harvest of 1917-1919 in unhappy Russia.

Macaulay was another great and far-seeing historian. He made almost a hundred years ago a prophecy concerning the young American republic:

"Your republic will be pillaged and ravaged in the twentieth century, just as the Roman Empire was by the Barbarians in the fifth century, with this difference, that the devastators of the Roman Empire came from abroad, while your Barbarians will be the people of your own country and the product of your own institutions."

God save our country from such a fate!

CHAPTER VIII

What Shall Be the End of these Things? The Final Conflict and the Coming Victory

What shall be the end of these things? This question was asked by the prophet Daniel some twenty-five hundred years ago after he had beheld the rise and fall of empires in his God-given visions. We look back over the history of almost six thousand years, a history of conflict, a history of wars and bloodshed, a history of human suffering and misery. Is this mournful history to continue? All attempts from the side of man in the past, to bring about a change, have failed. They are failing today. As we have seen, the process of an imagined evolution does not work. Civilization has failed and if the boasted remedies, socialism and communism, became universally applied, the promised Utopia would not come, but worse misery and disaster would follow. Past history and the present Russian conditions verify this fully. Is science going to give us light about a better future, about the dethronement of evil and the enthronement of righteousness? Is science going to stop the curse which is upon everything? We have seen science is unable to give us any satisfactory light on the origin of all things, and so it is unable to give us light on the future. As to the physical earth, scientists have ventured their guesses. Some say the earth will get colder and colder and finally become an icicle; another set of learned men think the earth will burn up and become a planet like the moon. So one may take his choice.

As the Bible gives us the trustworthy knowledge about creation, so it gives us knowledge about the future. The God who knows the end from the beginning has made the future known and through His chosen instruments, His prophets, has given in His Word the outcome of it all.

As the seed of the woman appeared once in humiliation for the bruising of the heel, that is to suffer and to die, so the same seed of the woman, who died and rose again must also carry out the second part of God's program, to bruise the serpent's head, that is to defeat him and gain the completest victory over the author of sin. This final defeat and coming victory is not achieved, according to the Word of God, in a spiritual way, so that gradually the overthrow of evil takes place, but it will be brought about by the personal return of the Lord Jesus Christ. The defeat of Satan in its finality, and the complete Victory of God, can only be brought about by that glorious coming event, when the Christ, who is now bodily present at the right hand of God, returns in person. No matter what creeds of different denominations teach, no matter what good men believe, this, and this alone is the teaching of Scripture.

Both Testaments give us the *political end of our age*. This is revealed in the second and seventh chapters of the Book of Daniel. In both chapters the world empires, which have dominion during the times of the Gentiles, beginning with Babylon and its king Nebuchadnezzar, are revealed. The fourth one is the Roman world empire. In its final form it is seen in the prophetic dream of the man image. This image reveals in its composition of the different metals the process of deterioration. Gold symbolizes the Babylonian empire; silver the empire which followed, the Medo-Persian. The next the Alexandrian empire is typified by brass and the fourth, the Roman empire, by iron. The two legs represent the East and West Roman divisions. Finally, the clay comes into prominence, though iron is still present in the ten toes of the feet. Clay is of the earth and does not mix with iron. Iron represents the monarchical form of government; clay the rule by the people. The political end of this age will consist in the abolition of governments by the rising of the people, the proletariat. They begin their reign while small kingdoms still persist. Then something happens. A stone falling from above demolishes the whole man-image by striking the feet. The stone becomes a mountain after having done its demolishing work and fills the whole earth. The stone which does this work is the prophetic picture of the return of Christ, verified by His own claims (Matt. xxi:

42-44). The mountain filling the earth is the symbol of His coming kingdom, in which He reigns as King.

The same age-ending is revealed to Daniel under the symbol of four beasts, which rise out of the sea of nations (Chapter vii). The first, the lion, is the symbol of the Babylonian empire; the second, the bear, symbolizes the Medo-Persian; the third the leopard, with wings and four heads, the Alexandrian and its four-fold division and the fourth beast is a great, terrible looking nondescript with ten horns. It is the symbol of the Roman empire in its final development, the ten horns correspond to the ten toes on the image. Here again is written the same process of evolution, not upward, but downward—from the noble lion to the horrible beast with iron teeth. The same degeneracy is expressed as in the metals of the image. But here is an additional feature. Amid the ten horns arises a little horn. Of this little horn we read that it is a person. "And he shall speak great words against the Most High, and shall wear out the Saints of the Most High, and think to change times and laws, and they (the times and laws) shall be given into his hand" (Dan. vii:25). This dreadful being is one of Satan's masterpieces through whom he will wage the final conflict. He will be the political domineering head of nations, which are once more united in the revived Roman empire. Then the scene changes. In the clouds of heaven, appears one like the Son of Man. He receives a worldwide kingdom, while the beasts and the little horn disappear and their dominion is ended. No Christian should be in doubt who this Son of Man is who receives the kingdoms of the world and through whom the evil reign of the serpent and his representatives will be forever ended. It is the same who told the highpriest, when He stood before him bound as a prisoner, "Henceforth ye shall see the Son of Man sitting at the right hand of power and *coming in the clouds of heaven*" (Matt. xxvii:64). It is Christ in His return to this earth.

In Revelation xiii the same final political condition of the end of the times of the Gentiles is seen. And here we read that the beast, the little horn, receives his power from the dragon, from Satan. He speaks great things of blasphemy, blasphemes God, His name and His dwelling place and those who dwell in heaven. He hates all who hold on to God and His truth (Rev. xiii:1-10).

For the sake of clearness we wish to state that the main theatre of all this will be Europe. That other nations, like ours, will be involved in some of these things seems to be certain, but the European countries will experience all this to the full.

As it is known to all students of prophecy, Russia is outside of the territory of the Roman empire and its future political revival. As we learned, Russia under Sovietism is the triumph of Marxism. The world revolution which Russia plans with the hatred against God and His Christ is all Satanic and is in full swing with the political end of the age, for it is this anti-Christian spirit which undermines other nations of Europe. But ultimately Russia under the leadership of a powerful head will associate herself with nations like Gomer (probably Germany), Togormah, Persia, Ethiopia, etc., and form a great alliance. It is interesting to see how this is being effected now, for the Red Republic is extending its domination into Central Asia and elsewhere. When finally the head arises, who is known in Scripture as the "king of the North" the hordes of God-defying nations will assemble themselves for a final conflict under the leadership of the serpent. All this is written in Ezekiel's prophecy (Chapters xxxviii:xxxix).

When one studies the European chaos as the result of the world war, hears of the attempts to unite Europe to restore the Roman Empire, and sees the rising of the people in democracies, and the onward rush into socialism and communism, one feels the time for the fulfillment of these things cannot be far away. All that is needed is the Satan-possessed, God-opposing leader, that little horn. He may be in the world already; only God knows who he is and where he is.

There is a Scripture which demands our attention. We give it in a corrected rendering:

"Now we beg you, brethren, by the coming of our Lord Jesus Christ and our gathering together unto Him, that ye be not soon shaken in mind, nor troubled, neither by spirit, nor by word, nor by letter, as if it came from us, as that the Day of the Lord is now at hand. Let no one deceive you in any manner, because (that day will not be) unless the apostasy have first come and the man of sin be revealed, the son of perdition; who opposes and exalts himself on high against all called God, or object of worship; so that he himself sits down in the temple of God, showing himself that he is God. Do ye not remember that, being yet with you, I said these things to you? And now ye know that which restrains, that he should be revealed in his own time. For the mystery of lawlessness already works only there is He who restrains now until he be gone, and then the lawless one shall be revealed, whom the Lord Jesus shall consume with the breath of His mouth and shall annul by the appearing of His coming; whose coming is according to the working of Satan in all power and signs and wonders of falsehood, and in all deceit of unrighteousness to them that perish, because they have not received the love of the truth that they might be saved" (2 Thess. ii:1-10).

This passage of Scripture reveals the final conflict of the age and shows also the final defeat of lawlessness. We must therefore examine it more closely.

The Thessalonian Christians, erstwhile heathen, like all apostolic Christians, lived in the joyful expectation of the return of Christ. "They waited for His Son from heaven, whom He raised from the dead, even Jesus, who delivereth us from the wrath to come" (1 Thess. i:10). Some one had disturbed them greatly in their simple faith and hope by circulating a rumor that the day of the Lord was then about to come. Evidently some one had used Paul's name as if he had sent them this information. Now the day of the Lord is that great day so often and so vividly described by the Old Testament prophets, on which the Lord is manifested in visible glory. In the New Testament our Lord spoke of the same day as being His day, the day of the Son

of Man, when every eye shall see Him, when He receives the
throne of His glory and when He judges the nations in
righteousness. The Apostles also speak of that day. It
is the day of the crushing of the serpent's head.

These false reports which circulated among the Thessalonians became the occasion of enlightening them, and us
as well, as to the conditions which precede that day, the
manifestation of lawlessness before that day comes, and
how that day will end the mystery of lawlessness.

The first thing the inspired Apostle shows must precede
that day is the *apostasy*. What is the apostasy and what
is an apostate? Apostasy is the departure from professed
principles. An apostate is a person who has forsaken his
faith or his party. To illustrate: Here is a certain well-
known teacher. He was active in Y. M. C. A. work; he
preached the great message of the Gospel of Jesus Christ,
that Christ died for our sins according to the Scriptures,
that He is the only way to God. He has abandoned it,
given it up, and is now a socialist, a friend of the Soviets.
That is an apostate. It is a fact verified by history that
an apostasy has been going on throughout this present age.
The Lord taught that such would be the case in the parable
of the enemy putting the evil seed into the same field in
which the wheat had been sown. The wheat and the tares
then grow together, the tares, as tares will do, crowding out
the wheat. Already, as stated before, apostasy manifested
itself in the beginning of the age. The beloved disciple
wrote of his own times, in his high old age, "There are many
antichrists." We have followed the increasing corruption
of sound doctrine through ritualism and the worst corruption through rationalism. As the age advances and draws
to its close there is an increase of apostasy. Our days
witness this.

In the passage we have quoted we read of *the* apostasy;
that is a different thing from *an* apostasy. It reveals the
fact that the age ends with a complete turning away from
revealed truth, with the denial of God and of Christ, that
this great apostasy will finally head up in the manifestation

of a great godless leader, called by the apostle the man of sin, the son of perdition. It is the final antichrist whose person and work is more fully described in Daniel xi:36 to 38, and Revelation xiii:11-18. From the latter passage we learn that he will be a counterfeit Christ for he has, in symbol, two horns like a lamb, but speaks as the dragon. Inasmuch as he comes out of the land he will arise from among the Jews. There are other reasons why this godless leader will be a Jew. His manifestation will be in Israel's land, as we shall show later; he will take a prominent place in the temple, the place of worship. He will be the false Messiah and King. All this necessitates a Jewish origin.

Here we must call attention to the fact that while there is an on-sweeping apostasy in Christendom, there is also a corresponding Jewish apostasy, or rather infidelity. Any Christian will honor the orthodox Old Testament believing Jews, who still cling to the hope of a coming Messiah, and who pray for His coming and expect him. They know the promises of the kingdom and the promises of a glorious future, yet there is upon them a judicial blindness. They keep their feasts year in and year out, generation after generation, hoping for the promised day when their wanderings among the nations of the world are ended and they can get back to the promised land.

But they are becoming less. The greater part of Jewry has become reformed, or as we call it "deformed." They no longer believe in the law and in the prophets. The Messiah and the glorious future is looked upon as a delusion. One of them said years ago—the Messiah we love is the dollar—Jerusalem we do not want, Washington is our Jerusalem. Turning away from the hope of their fathers and their own Scriptures, they become infidels and finally through their reaching out after material things and power they become a menace. The lower elements become lawless. As we have shown, these infidel Jews were prominent in the revolutionary propaganda during the nineteenth century. Karl Marx, the author of the "Communist Bible" was an infidel Jew; so was Lasalle and hundreds of others active in the socialistic-anarchistic and communistic activities. Trotzsky and at least two score other leaders of the Russian revolution were apostate Jews. They make themselves felt in our country and in other civilized countries. Watching the names of those who were arrested in anti-government demonstrations we find that a large percentage are Jews. We must mention another fact. Apostate Christians, by which we mean professing Christians, who have turned against supernatural Christianity, like Drs. Sherwood Eddy, Harry Emerson Fosdick and hundreds of others, fraternize with the rationalistic Jewish elements. They are bedfellows in socialistic organizations. There is a strange coming together; infidel preachers invite infidel Jews to their "pulpits" and reformed Jewish rabbis welcome modernistic preachers to their synagogues. The Religious "Book-Club" of New York, under the leadership of several outstanding modernists has recommended books, written by rationalistic Jews, to their "Christian" club members. It is an indication that as this age ends the infidel Gentile and Jewish forces will unite to make opposition to God and to His Christ, and when finally that man of sin appears, the antichrist, he will be accepted by the apostate Gentile-Christian, for he denies the Father and the Son, just what the apostate denies. The apostate denies the Deity of Jesus Christ, and it is written "whosoever denieth the Son hath not the Father." And the same man of sin will be acceptable to the Jew for he will deny "that Jesus is the Christ," the Messiah (1 John ii:18-23). He will be accepted by the infidel Jews as their Messiah. Jew and Gentile will then fulfill, through satanic delusion and power, what is written in the second psalm. Gentiles rage, people imagine vain things and finally there is a confederacy "against the Lord and against His anointed (the Christ)."

Of this coming head of the apostasy it is written that "he opposes and exalts himself on high against all called God, or object of veneration; so that he himself sits down in the temple of God, shewing himself that he is God." He, with his denial of the Father and the Son, and that Jesus is the Christ, takes the place of God and demands worship for himself. He proclaims himself as the Messiah mimicking Christ. Many commentaries, especially the older ones. also certain cults, like Seventh Day Adventism, teach that the man of sin is the papacy. But this is incorrect. The head of that great ritualistic system, which has corrupted the doctrine of Christ, does not deny the Father and the Son. Nor does the Pope deny that Jesus is the Christ. He claims to be the vice-regent of Christ on earth, but certainly not Christ Himself. We therefore dismiss this theory. The temple mentioned in which he appears and in which he demands worship is not at all the church, but it is a *Jewish temple*.

In the end of the age, while the manifestation of the author of sin in lawlessness and God opposition is world-wide, the final manifestation is narrowed down to Israel's land. It is there where the once rejected Christ will re-appear. He left from the Mount of Olives and to the same place will He come back (Zech. xiv:4). Jerusalem will come into prominence, for there the forces of lawlessness will gather under Satanic control and leadership. In Israel's land the real battle of Armageddon will take place. There the nations are gathered once more (Rev. xvi:16). The serpent knowing that his conqueror will appear in Israel's land with His heavenly army, will marshal his hosts, his seed, for the final conflict. John tells us, "I saw the beast (the little horn of Daniel, chapter vii) and the kings of the earth and their armies gathered together to make war against Him that sat upon the horse, and against His army" (Rev. xix:19). Then He appears in His majesty and glory. The symbolic stone of Nebuchadnezzar's dream vision strikes and the demolition takes place. Then also appear the hordes from the north, Gog and Magog. Their fate is prewritten in the Prophet Ezekiel (chapter xxxix). The victorious Christ will then lay hold on the serpent, Satan, the dragon, the devil and he will be stripped of his power, so that he can no longer deceive the nations (Rev. xx:1-3).

Preceding these attacks upon Jerusalem, when the last

siege takes place (see Zech. xiv) the man of sin, the Antichrist, will do his pernicious work in Jerusalem itself. There the last page of the ending age will be written. Jerusalem will be the great storm center of that predicted "great tribulation" with its horrors.

Some forty years ago there began in Judaism a significant national revival. Orthodox Jews always had in their hearts a homesickness for the land of their fathers, and sporadic efforts of colonization were made from time to time. Then arose a great leader, Dr. Theodore Herzl. He formulated a plan to establish a Jewish state in Palestine. Zionism was born and as a result there has been for many years a revival of the Jewish national hope. But the Zionistic movement was not the product of faith in God's oath-bound covenants. It is not the result of a spiritual revival, a return to God. It was and it is still a movement of unbelief, a political and humanitarian scheme, which has no use for the real Jewish hope, which centers in the promised Messiah King. When the unspeakable Turk, that monstrous Sultan was reigning, the man who has rightly been called "the damned," for he instituted the horrible persecutions of the Armenian Christians, Dr. Herzl, who had approached him with an offer to purchase Palestine, said, "If your Majesty makes our national aspirations possible we shall look upon you as our Messiah." Nothing came of it, for it is written, "The land shall not be sold for it is mine" (Lev. xxxv:23).

Herzl died quite young, but the national hope did not die with him. Then came the world war. One of the greatest results was the ending of the Turk's rule, or rather, misrule, of Palestine. Jerusalem was captured by General Allenby and put under British mandate. Since that time an astonishing progress has been made in Israel's land. Thousands of Jews have gathered from the four corners of the earth, so that today over 200,000 are living in Palestine, more than ever before since the destruction of Jerusalem 70 A.D., and thousands more are waiting to settle there. Great agricultural schemes, irrigation and other improvements, have been brought about. New industries are being established, a university is now located there and the Hebrew language is revived, and is once more a living language. As Ezekiel saw in his great prophetic vision, there is a stir among the dry bones of the house of Israel (Ezek. xxxvii) An organization is effected, but the life-giving Spirit is lacking. He is not there because all the schemes and plans do not come from faith in God's Word. The whole movement is one of unbelief, which is displeasing to God, and finally results in new judgments upon Israel's land.

One of the schemes now advocated is the restoration of the temple worship as demanded by the levitical code. They speak of building a temple, and it is said that young men, who trace their descent from Levi, are being instructed in the different ceremonials. One can readily see, that, in order to consummate the restoration plans, another temple is needed. It will come to pass some day, and when it does it will be the culmination of Jewish unbelief, and will bring upon them the indignation of Jehovah, the God of Israel.

This is strikingly indicated in the last chapter of the Prophet Isaiah, which deals with the days of the Jews restoration in unbelief. We must glance at it. The chapter begins with the statement of building a house for the Lord. "Where is the house that ye build unto Me? and where is the place of My rest?" In the third verse the future sacrifices are anticipated. In the places of worship during Old Testament times, lambs, bulls and goats were brought as sacrifices, because the new and living way into God's holy presence was not yet made. All the sacrifices and offerings were prophecies of the true sacrifice and that precious blood which the holy Son of God was to shed as the Lamb of God. To reject Him and His sacrificial work is now the crowning sin, and for Jews to turn back to these sacrifices, which have no more meaning, is doubly obnoxious in the sight of God. We hear Him speak in this prophecy about this consummating act of Jewish unbelief. "He that killeth an ox (in sacrifice) is as if he slew a man; he that sacrificeth a lamb, as if he cut off a dog's neck; he that offereth an oblation, as if he offered swine's blood; he that burneth incense, as if he blessed an idol. Yea, they have chosen their own ways, and their soul delighteth in their abominations" (Isa. lxvi:4). Read on in this chapter and find how, when this abomination is in Jerusalem, the Lord will come and by His sudden manifestation end this false worship.

Into this temple of unbelief and abomination the man of sin will come to take his place there, claiming that he is the Messiah-King, and then demand in his blasphemous exaltation the worship which is due to God and Christ. In the first part of His prophetic Olivet Discourse our Lord gives the picture of the last seven years of this age and what will happen in Jerusalem. He speaks of the abomination of desolation and warns the godly remnant of His earthly people Israel.

"When ye therefore shall see the abomination of desolation, spoken of by Daniel, the prophet, stand in the holy place—whoso readeth let him understand—then let them which be in Judea flee into the mountains" (Matt. xxiv:15-16). The passage to which our Lord refers is found in Daniel xi:36. "And the king (the false Messiah—antichrist) shall do according to his will; he shall exalt himself above every god, and shall speak marvelous things against the God of gods, and shall prosper till the indignation be accomplished for that that is determined shall be done. Neither shall he regard the God of his fathers (his Jewish fathers) nor the desire of women, nor regard any god, for he shall magnify himself above all." This fully harmonizes with the text in 2 Thessalonians ii:4: "who opposes and exalts himself above all that is called God, or object of veneration; so that he himself sits down in the temple of God, shewing himself that he is God."

Antiochus Epiphanes in the second century before Christ, as also predicted by Daniel (chapter viii), defiled the temple, but here is a greater defilement. Satan's masterpiece sits there, endowed with all his powers. He works lying miracles (as he does already in certain anti-Christian cults). It is the working of Satan. A strong delusion has come and those who did not receive the love of the truth for their salvation will readily accept the final lie of the serpent. Infidel Jews and apostate Christians are included for Satan's strong delusion will then be heralded all over the world. "And he doeth great wonders so that he maketh fire come down from heaven on the earth in the sight of men, and deceiveth them that dwell on the earth by the means of those miracles which he had power to do in the sight of the beast, saying to them that dwell on the earth that they should make an image to the beast, which had the wound by the sword and did live. And he had power to give life unto the image of the beast, that the image of the beast should both speak, and cause that as many as would not worship the image of the beast should be killed" (Rev. xiii:13-15).*

All this shows that Satan and his angels will manifest their power at the very close of the age. The mystery of lawlessness, which has worked from the very beginning of man's history, is reaching its consummation in the final seven years of our age. The reader perhaps would like to know why we mention seven years. The answer is found in the Book of Daniel and in Revelation. The seven years constitute the last prophetic week of the prophecy which Gabriel brought to Daniel. †

We have to examine next another great statement in the Thessalonian text. Twice the Spirit of God speaks of something which *restrains*, which keeps back the full manifestation of this mystery of lawlessness. We read "that which restrains" and "there is He who restrains now until He be gone, and then that lawless one shall be revealed." In other words the final phase of the conflict of the ages, the manifestation of the lawless one, who is the incarnation of Satan, all the prophecies concerning that final conflict, such as the great tribulation, the judgments which will be executed on the earth, cannot take place till the restraining power, the restraining one (a person) is removed.

Who has the power to keep back the final, horrible scenes of God-defiance, atheism and the destruction of human

---

*See the author's exposition of Revelation.
†See the author's exposition of Daniel IX.

government? Who restrains the serpent from making its final, last strike at God and His Christ?

We believe the history of the past gives us an answer. Who has curbed evil in its various forms? What power was it, which preserved the Church of Jesus Christ during the Roman persecutions? Who brought the truth back from the Romish superstitions? Who instituted the reformation so that Satan was checked in his aims? Why did Satan not succeed through the Illuminati and through the French revolution? Who curbed the serpent's attempt to head up all these things in the final onslaught? Why have his repeated attempts to destroy the Church and the Truth of God miscarried? How is it that with all the hate expressed against the Church, the Church instead of being weakened, grows? How is it that even in Soviet Russia with its hordes of godless men and women the Gospel persists and continues to have its triumphs? What is the explanation of all this? We answer, *the presence of the Holy Spirit on Earth*.

The true Church of Jesus Christ, composed of all true believers, is a divine organism, which had its beginning on the day of Pentecost, when the Holy Spirit of God came to earth. With His coming the great spiritual work of this age was inaugurated. The apostles with all other believers were by Him united into the body of Christ, the Church, each member being possessed and filled with the Spirit. The Church became thus "the habitation of God through the Spirit" (Ephes. ii:22). This work is continued by the Spirit of God during this age. The great message of the Gospel is preached in every continent and through that message the members of the body of Christ are gathered and added to that body. So long as this work of the Holy Spirit is unfinished, so long as the great purpose of God in this age is unaccomplished, the mystery of lawlessness cannot have its culmination in the apostasy and in the manifestation of the lawless one. *The Holy Spirit has throughout this age been the restrainer. The power which has restrained the serpent's power is the power of the Spirit of God.*

Whenever the forces of evil attempted to reach their full manifestation the Spirit of God restrained them from reaching the goal. The entire history of the Church bears witness to this supernatural power.

But this work of the Spirit in gathering the body of Christ through the preaching of the Gospel message will not continue *ad infinitum*. It will come to an end. The Spirit of God will finish the work He came to do, for the body of Christ is an elect body, and some day it will be completed. What will happen then?

We look again at the quoted words from the Thessalonian epistle. Paul wrote, "We beg you, brethren, by the coming of our Lord Jesus Christ, *and our gathering together unto Him.*" What gathering together unto Him does Paul mean? The Church of Jesus Christ is not a permanent institution on this earth. Her destiny is not here, but in the heavenlies. The Head, the risen Christ is in glory, and all the members of His body must be united to the Head; the Bridegroom is in the Father's house, and some day the Bride must be brought to Him for the heavenly nuptials, when she will become the Lamb's wife (Rev. xix:6-9). When Paul speaks of the gathering together unto Him, he means the home gathering of all the redeemed. Of this great event this man of God received a special revelation. Well has it been termed "that blessed hope." We find it in the first Thessalonian epistle.

"For this we say unto you by the Word of the Lord, that we which are alive and remain unto the coming of the Lord shall not precede them which are asleep. For the Lord Himself shall descend from heaven with a shout, with the voice of the archangel, and with the trump of God; and the dead in Christ shall rise first; then we which are alive shall be caught up together with them in clouds, to meet the Lord in the air, and so shall we ever be with the Lord" (1 Thess. iv:15-17).

This is the gathering together unto Him. It will happen some day, literally as it is written. This is the end of true Christianity on the earth; the end of Christendom is something entirely different. This is the future of the true

Church of Christ. The Holy Spirit who indwells the Church will be needed for this coming event. By His power the bodies of the saints of God, who died in Christ will be quickened, and His power will change living believers in a moment, in the twinkling of an eye. This we find written in Romans viii:11, "But if the Spirit of Him that raised up Jesus from the dead dwell in you, He that raised up Christ from the dead shall also quicken (make alive) your mortal bodies by His Spirit who dwelleth in you." He is also needed with His power to carry the redeemed hosts through the heavens and bring them face to face with Christ, the Lord. The Spirit's work being finished, He holds His ascension when the Saints of God are gathered unto Him.

"*He who restrains now until He be gone.*" The meaning is clear, with the completed Church brought into the presence of the Lord, the Restrainer will be gone—*and then* the apostasy and the lawless one, *and then* the full manifestation of the mystery of lawlessness, *and then* the serpent's wrath, the serpent's final hiss and final work, for he knows his time is short (Rev. xii:12).

What it will mean when the Restrainer is no longer here, what it will mean when God's children no longer pray and witness, no longer reach out for the unsaved, we cannot even imagine.

All this is revealed in the last book of the New Testament, in the Patmos vision of the aged John. The removal of the true Church from earth to heaven is symbolically seen in the beginning of the fourth chapter, followed by the worship scenes in glory. After the Saints are in His presence the seven sealed book is opened and beginning with the sixth chapter we have a description of what will happen on the earth in the days when the lawless one is here. There will be judgments from above and the last three years and a half will be the great tribulation, which Daniel mentions (Dan. xii:1-3), which our Lord says will be sweeping the earth immediately before His visible return.

This exposition of the Restrainer and His restraining power in the removal of the Church, is questioned by some. The argument against it is on account of the Saints, who are mentioned during the time of trouble and tribulation, who are suffering in the coming world-revolution and world-chaos, whom the lawless one hates and tries to exterminate. If the true Church is removed from the earth, who are these suffering Saints? Are the modernists being converted? Are the evolutionists turning to Christ? That a multitude of people will come out of the great tribulation and be saved is verified by the Scriptures, but they are not those who rejected the Gospel, nor are they added to the Church, for the Church, as the body of Christ is completed.

During those days of Satanic manifestation and power, before the end of the age comes, "this Gospel of the kingdom (that the King is about to return to earth with His power as Judge) shall be preached in all the world as a witness unto all nations" (Matt. xxiv). So there will be a great witness given during the final years, during the days when the mystery of lawlessness has reached its goal. The nations which never heard the Gospel of Grace will hear the witness about the coming King and with it the call to repent.

But this brings other questions. If the true Church is gone who is going to do the preaching? Who is going to give the message? Certainly not the modernistic-socialistic-communistic preachers. Who is going to give the witness? And if the Holy Spirit is gone, how can these witnesses have success with their message and how can people repent and believe the final call?

The witnesses will be Israelites of the different tribes. They are the sealed company in Revelation vii. Here again we must be clear as to their identity. They will not be the international Jews, the political-financial schemers, the lawless elements, who ridicule and hate religion of any kind and are atheists. These Jews will worship the beast. They reject the true Christ and accept the false Messiah. Our Lord predicted this. "I am come in My Father's name, and ye receive me not, if another shall come in his own name, him ye will receive" (John v:43).

The orthodox Jews, who have held on to the faith of their fathers, who pray for the coming of the Messiah-King,

whose eyes are blinded that they cannot see, from them
the veil will be removed. The Holy Spirit after having
finished His work in connection with the body of Christ,
begins His work with the remnant of Israel. Their **eyes**
are opened. It dawns upon them that the long-expected
King is about to come. The fulness of the Gentiles has
come in and their blindness is ended (Rom. xi:26). They
receive the knowledge that the rejected One, the Lord
Jesus Christ, is the coming King. They begin to pray
prayers prewritten by the Spirit of God (See Psa. lxxx:17-19;
Isa. lxiii:15-lxiv:1-8). When the man of sin appears they
refuse his lying signs and wonders, they refuse him worship,
as Mordecai refused to bow the knee before Haman. They
have to suffer persecution and many of them will be killed.
The twelfth chapter in Revelation tells us about this. "And
the dragon (the devil) was wroth with the woman (Israel)
and went to make war with the remnant of her seed (the
God-fearing Jews and Israelites), which keep the command-
ments of God, and have the testimony of Jesus" (Rev.
xii:17).   The seed of the woman faces for the last time
the serpent and his seed. And this remnant sealed will give
the witness to all the nations, the witness of the coming
King. They are well fitted to do this, for they are found
among all nations and speak their languages.

And the Holy Spirit, the Restrainer will, as He did in Old
Testament times, be with this godly remnant of Jews,
sustain them in their work and those of the Gentile nations
who believe their witness will also be under His power and
guidance, so that they can overcome. On the other hand
He will permit the power of the serpent to do its utmost
in God-defiance and lawlessness till the hour of defeat
arrives.

In our text the defeat is expressed in these words—"Whom
the Lord shall consume with the breath of His mouth and
shall annul by the appearing of His coming." Needless
to say the One who will defeat the serpent and his seed is
the Lord Jesus Christ. The crushing defeat comes when
He returns in great power and glory. How vividly this is
revealed in numerous prophecies. We quote but one, the

Second Psalm. The raging nations, raging under Satanic control, the confederacies of rulers, raving against God and against His Christ, trying to break their bands and get rid of their cords, give a prophetic picture of the final conflict. Heaven is silently looking on; God above it all holds them in derision. But the scene changes. "Then shall He speak unto them in His wrath, and vex them in His sore displeasure. Yet have I set My King upon My holy hill of Zion. I will declare the decree; the Lord has said unto Me, Thou art My Son, this day have I begotten Thee. Ask of Me and I will give Thee the nations for Thine inheritance and the uttermost parts of the earth for Thy possession. Thou shalt break them with a rod of iron; Thou shalt dash them in pieces like a potter's vessel."

The most glorious vision of His return is recorded in the nineteenth chapter of Revelation (verses ii-16). The white horse He rides is the symbol of victory; the names He bears are telling out His majestic greatness. He has a name written, which is known only to Him—the Name of His Deity; in incarnation His name is the "Word of God" and the future name, which He claims with His return is "King of kings and Lord of lords." Then follows the complete dethronement of the powers of evil and lawlessness. Satan is bound to deceive the nations no more.

His victorious return will mean much more besides the defeat of the serpent and its seed. It will end all infidelity; it will be a complete vindication of His Person as it will be a vindication of the Bible as the infallible revelation of God; it will demonstrate that His Word is true from the beginning. And more than that the victorious Seed of the woman, the Son of Man coming in His glory, will solve all the problems with which humanity is wrestling today; He will institute the government of righteousness and peace; He will bring to the nations the true liberty, fraternity and equality; He will end conflict between capital and labor for "He shall judge the poor with righteousness" and "He shall save the poor and the needy" (Psa. lxxii). He will bring universal disarmament, "for He shall speak peace unto the nations and His dominion shall be from sea to sea, and from the

river even unto the uttermost parts of the earth" (Zech.
ix:10). He will bring deliverance for groaning creation for
"the wolf shall dwell with the lamb, and the leopard shall
lie down with the kid, and the calf and the young lion and
the fatling together, and a little child shall lead them" (Isa.
xi:6). He who bore the crown of thorns on His bleeding
brow, the thorns, the emblem of the curse, will take away
the curse and "as it was in the beginning so it shall be."

Enthroned as King, He will have with Him His seed, His
glorified Saints who reign and rule with Him in the new
creation, when finally there will be a new heaven and a new
earth. Reader—will you be there?

> "Come then and added to Thy many crowns
> Receive yet one, the crown of all the earth,
> Thou who alone art worthy! It was Thine
> By ancient covenant ere nature's birth,
> And Thou hast made it Thine by purchase since,
> And overpaid its value in Thy blood.
> Thy Saints proclaim Thee King, and in their hearts
> Thy title is engraven with a pen
> Dipt in the fountain of eternal love.
> Thy Saints proclaim Thee King; and Thy delay
> Gives courage to their foes, who, could they see
> The Dawn of Thy last Advent long desired,
> Would creep into the bowels of the hills,
> And flee for safety to the falling rocks.
> The very spirit of the world is tired
> Of its own daunting question asked so long—
> Where is the promise of our Lord's approach?
> The infidel has shot his bolts away,
> Till his exhausted quiver yielding none,
> He gleans the blunted shafts that have recoiled,
> And aims them at the shield of Truth again.
>   *   *   *   *   *
> Come then and added to Thy many crowns
> Receive yet one, as radiant as the rest,
> Due to Thy last and most effectual work,
> Thy Word fulfilled, the conquest of the world."*

"He who testifieth these things saith, Surely I come
quickly. Amen! Even so Come Lord Jesus" (Rev. xxii:20).

*"The Task," W. Cowper.

MARANATHA.

CHAPTER IX

THE COMING GREAT EVENT

The coming great event in human history will be most wonderful and startling. No pen can fully describe it; no mind can imagine what it will be and what it will mean to all the world. The event will not be a new and great discovery before which all previous discoveries pale into insignificance. Nor will it be a great invention, which produces mighty changes, nor anything else that man does.

The next great event will be the manifestation of the Super-Man. For years the world has been speaking of the coming of a super-man. Artists have painted imaginary pictures of him, with a high forehead, showing super-intelligence, attractive face, indicating his moral and sweet disposition. Poets have sung his praises and imagined what the coming super-man would accomplish in the betterment of the race. Eugenics, new educational schemes, hygenics, and different sciences are attempting the production of such a super-man. But he has not made his appearance yet. We are still waiting for the super-man to spring from the race. If he should come, and through him the race should be lifted to a higher plane, the man-made laws of evolution would be scientifically proved correct and unimpeachable. But the super-man of whom the world dreams, whom poets sing, and artists picture and model in clay, will never come forth from the human race. The super-man is an idle hopeless dream. Sin, disease and death, these laws which govern human existence, not like evolution, a hypothesis, but unalterable facts, shatter the dream of the super-man.

Yet there *is* a Super-Man, one who is above all and over all. There is a Super-Man, not a spirit or a phantom, but a real Man with a human body. This Super-Man is

The Lord Jesus Christ.

The coming great event in human history is the visible and glorious manifestation of the Son of Man, the Super-Man, far above all principalities and powers, and every name that is named; the Super-Man who has all power in heaven and on earth; the Super-Man whose are the crown rights over all the earth.

The Super-Man is the Son of God. He became Man not by natural generation, but by the supernatural process of the virgin birth, He was conceived by the Holy Spirit. The life He lived on earth demonstrates the fact of His super-humanity. His own witness was, "I am from above . . . I am not of this world" (John viii:23). He was sinless, holy and undefiled. No flaw has ever been found in His life and character; nor was there one. He towers above the rest of humanity. The words He spoke and the works He did are the credentials of His Deity. And this wonderful person, the God-Man, came to die a sacrificial death. He died as the Lamb of God, and then conquered death and the grave in His triumphant resurrection from among the dead. Through Him humanity can be lifted from sin and death, and become also super-human. Those who believe on Him, accept Him as their Saviour, who died for their sins, are born again. In this new birth they receive the nature from above and with it eternal life. Like Himself they are then "from above and not of this world" (John xvii:14). Believers, in their spiritual nature, are super-human beings. Sin, death and the grave are for them conquered foes.

And Christ, the Son of Man, the Super-Man, the mighty victor over Satan, sin, death and the grave, is in heaven at the right hand of God, as the head of a new humanity, the new creation. He who existed in the form of God, exists now in the form of Man, risen from the dead and glorified. This Super-Man, in whom the fulness of the Godhead dwells bodily, who lived a brief life on this earth, who has been and is the most tremendous factor and power in all history, the same One will come once more into human history. This second coming will be the most wonderful and the most startling event of the future.

The Certainty of It

Future history is uncertain. Many times men have tried

to forecast future political events and failed in it. No one knows if the government of the United States is going to continue as it is now; nor does any one know for certain that France will remain a Republic, or that Mussolini will succeed in reviving the dominion and glory of the Roman Empire. All future events in human history are shrouded in mystery. While it is true, "history repeats itself," no one knows how and when it will happen, or what new forms the repetition of history will take on. But there is a way by which man can know the future. There is a knowledge put at the door of the human race, which is trustworthy, because it is infallible. It is knowledge given by revelation of the omniscient Spirit of God, and this knowledge is found in the Bible, the Word of God.

The Bible forecasts the future. Its forecasts are sure and certain beyond the shadow of even the remotest doubt. History proves it. Hundreds of years before certain empires came into existence, the Bible predicted their coming and what should come to pass. This we find in the prophecies of Daniel. Other prophets of God foretold the fall and utter ruin of Babylon and Nineveh, when these cities were flourishing and in the zenith of their power. Egypt's history is prewritten in the Word of God and all was minutely fulfilled. Still more striking is the pre-written history of the people Israel. This fact no infidel has ever been able, nor will be able, to answer. Fulfilled prophecy demonstrates the Bible as the infallible Word of God.

The crown of all Bible prophecy is what is written concerning the Messiah, promised to the people Israel. For many centuries His coming was announced. "When the fulness of the time (the appointed time) was come, God sent forth His Son, made of a woman, made under the law" (Gal. iv:4). He came as the second Man, made a little lower than the angels, the Holy One, the Super-Man. His birth, His life, His words, His works, His sufferings, His sacrificial death, His burial, His physical resurrection, His ascension and His presence at the right hand of God, confirm what the prophets had spoken, for all these events were literal fulfilments of their predictions. Still one great line of prophecy given by the same man of God, who spoke and wrote as they were moved by the Holy Spirit, remains to be fulfilled. These are the prophecies which announce His second coming in power and visible glory, the prophecies which predict His enthronement as King, surrounded by the heavenly hosts, and His reign as the Prince of Peace. There was no failure in the accomplishment of the predictions relating to His coming in humiliation; there can be no failure in the fulfilment of His glorious return. The absolute certainty of it is assured.

He Was Not Mistaken

It is a common statement, found among the liberals in Protestant Christendom, that the Lord Jesus Christ in saying certain things, was mistaken. They speak of Him as if He was ignorant of certain facts, or that He accommodated Himself to the mistaken beliefs of the Jews. All these dishonoring expressions are the results of disbelief in the God-Man, the infallible Son of God and infallible Son of Man. Those who walked with Him, and talked with Him, testified, "Thou knowest all things." Could He who is the Truth Himself speak that which is not true? Or could He endorse error? Whatever He spoke and taught is infallibly true. He was not mistaken in anything.

He was not mistaken when He announced that after His passion, after His resurrection and ascension, He would come back to earth again the second time. Majestically, though bound, He stood before the high priest and answered his question—"tell us whether Thou be the Christ, the Son of God." "Thou hast said; nevertheless I say unto you, Hereafter shall ye see the Son of Man sitting on the right hand of power, and coming in the clouds of heaven" (Matt. xxvi:64). Many times before He had spoken in His teachings and parables of His return. He had comforted His grief-stricken disciples, when He had announced His departure from them, that they would soon be orphaned, by promising, "I will come again and receive you unto myself that where I am ye may be also" (John xiv:3). What He said about this coming in glory is in fullest harmony with the unfulfilled prophecies as to the same event. No, He was not mistaken when He announced His return to this earth on which He lived, on which He died, in which His body rested for a little while, and which He left as the risen, glorified Super-Man. Nor has His Church been mistaken in looking and waiting for Him to redeem His promise.

It is true, centuries have come and gone, and the longing expectation of His people has not been realized. It is true the heavens have been silent; they are silent today. But it cannot be thus for all time. That silence will be broken and the hope and expectation of His waiting people will be gloriously consummated.

To this we add, that all Christian doctrines are vitally linked with this great, coming event. The whole system of these doctrines demands His return. Christian service, the Christian's life, his walk, his hope of resurrection, the re-union with loved ones, and much else, cannot be detached from His return. It is one of the great truths of Christianity. Therefore, it is sure and certain. Nothing can be as sure and certain as the re-appearing of the Son of Man on this earth. He will surely come, and be revealed in His power and glory, when once more the appointed time comes. When that time arrives it will bring the consummating event of the ages; His visible, personal and glorious manifestation is the great coming event.

What It Will Mean

Historians often have found it hard to give an adequate description of some great events, or history making epochs in the drama of human existence. Historians who were eye-witnesses of battles, or the triumphal returns of victorious armies, spoke of what they beheld as indescribable. Though we read in the Scriptures of Truth the events of that coming day of all days, and prophetic vision acquaints us with what will take place, the finite mind cannot fully grasp it, nor can any human pen picture this great coming event. It is indescribable and transcends the most vivid imagination. What will it mean when heaven above opens and a glory light bursts forth, before which our sun pales, when heaven and earth shake, and He suddenly appears? What will it mean when once more the feet of the Son of Man touch this earth and He comes back to the place where He suffered and died? What will it mean when He receives the many diadems, and the throne of His glory, to reign henceforth as King of kings, and Lord of lords? What will it mean when he manifests in a sin-cursed, ruined creation His almighty redemption power? What will it mean?

It will mean the complete defeat of His enemies and their eternal silence. Never before in the history of Christendom has the question, "What think ye of Christ?" been such a burning question as it is now in our approach of the middle of the Twentieth Century. Books upon books are written about or Lord, generally under the name of "Jesus," "The Man of Galilee," or some other name. His blessed life is being commercialized. One writes "The Life of Christ," and this one is a bigotted Romanist. Another writes a puerile volume on "The Man Nobody Knows," a book which has next to no literary value. Still another modernist writes a new life of Christ, and a Reformed Jew produces "The Story of the Son of Man." Then there are motion pictures, passion plays and theatrical pageants, all depicting Him. And the writers get rich by their unscriptural descriptions of Him, who had not where to lay His head. But all dishonor His blessed, holy and worthy Name.

Worse still are the opinions expressed among those who use His name, and who claim to believe on Him. Thousands deny His Virgin-birth; they speak of Him as a philosopher, a religious leader, a socialist, a fine specimen of manhood, and as a good example to follow. His substitutionary suffering and death is denied; they do not believe that He ever rose physically from the dead. They sneer at the idea that there is a local heaven and that the Christ is seated there upon a throne. The Christ of modernism is the complete denial of the supernatural Christ of the Bible. These denials are crystallized in powerful movements. They are found in all evangelical denominations and their leading educational institutions. Instead of diminishing, these denials increase. They threaten now to sweep everything before them. There is but a small remnant which is true and faithful to the true Christ, the Son of the living God. The confusion is appalling and many ask, how will it end? Oh! it will end! And the end will be the complete defeat of His enemies. His manifestation will silence every mouth and will for ever prove that Peter was right, and the true Church was right, in believing and confessing, "Thou art the Christ, the Son of the living God!" Such systems as Christian Science, Modernism, Unitarianism, and all the Christ rejecting systems and cults will suddenly terminate with that great coming event, the return of the glorified Son of Man.

It will mean the glory of the Church, the Body of Christ. The Church, the true Church before this great coming event bursts upon the world, will be translated to meet the Lord in the air. This is fully revealed in 1 Thessalonians iv:13-18. Every member of that body will then be changed into the image of the Firstborn. The Son of God and the Son of Man will bring then His many sons unto glory. He will be glorified in them, while the whole body will be glorified with Him. The Church will share His glorious inheritance; the Saints will rule with Him over the earth.

It will mean the end of Gentile world rule. The times of the Gentiles continue till He returns. His return will mean the passing away of the present world government, whether it is autocracy, monarchy or the rule by the people and for the people. Both forms of human government, the one-man government or the people's government, are represented in the two feet of Nebuchadnezzar's dream-image (Dan. ii). The smiting stone is Christ's return. The stone ends every form of government as it is in existence now.

It will mean judgment for the wicked. He comes to judge and to punish according to His righteousness. He comes "in flaming fire taking vengeance on them that know not God, and that obey not the gospel of our Lord Jesus Christ; who shall be punished with everlasting destruction from the presence of the Lord, and from the glory of His power"

(2 Thess. i:8, 9).   All the enemies of Christ, the apostate, among the Gentiles and the Jews will face Him as Judge in that great coming event.

It will mean the conversion of the remnant of Israel.   When this great event arrives and He is manifested, Israel's hope will be realized.   They shall look upon Him, whom they pierced, and know Him by the prints of the nails in His hands.   All the promises made to them as a nation will then be made good.   The national blood-guiltiness will be wiped away; He will forgive their sins and remember them no more.   A nation will be born in a day.   The Spirit will be poured out upon them and they all shall know the Lord from the least to the greatest.   They will be gathered from all the countries of the earth.   Their land will become Immanuel's glorious land and Jerusalem will be a praise in the whole earth, for it is the City of the great King.

It will mean the establishment of His Kingdom on the earth and the conversion of the world.   He will receive in that day the throne of His father David and the throne over all the earth.   He asks the Father and He gives Him the nations for His inheritance and the uttermost parts of the earth for His possession.   The universe hears the never ending shout, "The kingdoms of this world are become the kingdom of our Lord, and His Christ; and He shall reign for ever and ever"— "Hallelujah, the Omnipotent reigneth."   He reigns from sea to sea and His glory covers the earth as the waters the sea.

It will mean the binding of Satan.   The Super-Man from heaven, the seed of the woman, when this great coming event has arrived will put His heel upon the serpent's head.   The enemy's complete overthrow has come.   He is bound to deceive the nations no more.   All idolatry and every form of wickedness which flourishes now will end.   Righteousness will be for ever enthroned.

It will mean Peace on Earth.   All peace treaties, disarmament pacts and national agreements cannot bring permanent peace for this peace-less world.   Nor can nations, by legislation or education, be taught to learn war no more.   "Peace on Earth" comes with the coming of the Prince of Peace.

Then nations will learn war no more and turn their swords into plowshares and their spears into pruning hooks. He only can speak peace to the nations and hush the national strifes as He hushed the waves of the Galilean Sea.

It will mean the banishment of oppression, of poverty, of famines and of pestilences. The King upon the throne will rule the world in righteousness. No longer will the hire of the laborer be kept by fraud; no longer will the greater part of the race struggle on in poverty; no longer will famines and pestilences sweep their millions away into untimely graves. The King is righteous. The King upon the throne is almighty. In His humiliation He showed His power over disease; He showed His power in satisfying the poor with bread, so that their hunger was stilled. Oh! the blessing He brings when He has received His own throne and rules in righteousness with all power in heaven and on earth!

It will mean the removal of the curse which rests on all creation. "For the earnest expectation of the creature waiteth for the manifestation of the sons of God. For the creature was made subject to vanity, not willingly, but by reason of Him who hath subjected the same in hope, because the creature itself also shall be delivered from the bondage of corruption into the glorious liberty of the children of God. For we know that the whole Creation groaneth and travaileth in pain together until now" (Rom. viii:19-22). "The wolf shall dwell with the lamb, and the leopard shall lie down with the kid, and the calf and the young lion and the fatling together, and a little child shall lead them. And the cow and the bear shall feed; their young ones shall lie down together; and the lion shall eat straw like the ox" (Is. xi:6-7). The curse which rests upon creation now will then be removed. No more devastating floods, hurricanes and storms! No more earthquakes and other physical disasters! Creation's Lord and Redeemer is upon the throne.

Such is the great coming event and what this event, His visible and glorious return, will mean. But not the half of it has been told.

CHAPTER X

THE COMING CREED

The creeds have gone, so speaks the age,
   The era of the sects is past.
Forward!   In spite of saint or sage,
   True freedom has begun at last.

The Christ of God is now no more;
   The Christ of man now sits supreme;
The cross is part of mythic lore,
   The resurrection morn a dream.

The age's progress fears no God,
   No righteous law, no Judge's throne;
Man bounds along his new found road,
   And calls the Universe his own.

Not faith in God, but faith in man,
   Is pilot now, and sail, and oar:
The creeds are shrivelled, cold, and wan;
   The Christ that has been is no more!

Old truths, which once struck deep in hearts,
   Fights hard for life, but fights in vain;
Old error into vigor starts,
   And fable comes to life again.

Old misbelief becomes earth's creed;
   The falsehood lives, the truth has died;
Man leans upon a broken reed,
   And falls in helplessness of pride.

He spurns the hand that would have led,
   The lips that would have spoken love:
The Book that would his soul have fed,
   And taught the wisdom from above.

The ever-standing cross, to him,
 Is but a Hebrew relic vain;
The wondrous birth at Bethlehem
 A fiction of the wandering brain.

He wants no Saviour and no light;
 No teacher but himself he needs;
He knows not of a human night,
 Save from the darkness of the creeds.

Eternal light hide not Thy face;
 Eternal Truth, direct our way;
Eternal Love, shine forth in grace,
 Reveal *our* darkness and *Thy* day.

When Horatius Bonar wrote this hymn almost sixty-five years ago he spoke as a prophet. Not much of the present day modernistic apostasy was known in that day. This poem gives a true description of the liberal creed so universal in the Twentieth Century.